THE POWER OF PRAYER PROPHECY AND PRAISE

Jamal E. Quinn

I0170394

A publication of ML Excellence

Table of Contents

DEDICATION

This book is dedicated to my LORD and Savior Jesus Christ who has given me great grace to write this book. I also thank the Holy Spirit who leads us and guides into all truth, and has given me spiritual wisdom, knowledge and understanding as it relates to prayer, prophecy and praise.

To all the believers in the Body of Christ that understand and acknowledge the importance and power of prayer, prophecy and praise!

To all the men and women of God over the years who taught me the importance of prayer, prophesied over my life, and gave me an opportunity to sing and praise the LORD! God bless you!

To my wife Sheryl and all the faithful Firm Foundation members who labor and serve faithfully with me in the work of the ministry! May God bless you richly!

Last but definitely not least, I want to dedicate this book to my late mother Mary Lillian Quinn who passed away at the age of 28, on Oct 9, 1973. The precious moments I spent with her as a sick child has blessed my life to this very day, with memories that will never be forgotten.

INTRODUCTION

All throughout the Bible there are three powerful spiritual weapons that have enabled the people of God to get the victory despite trials, tribulations, troubles, temptations and the attacks of the enemy. They are prayer, prophecy and praise.

The Bible says that a threefold cord is not easily broken in Ecclesiastes 4:12. These three powerful weapons of our warfare are not carnal, but mighty in God to the pulling down of strongholds according to 2 Corinthians 10:4.

We live in a time where every believer should understand the power of persistent prayer, powerful prophecy, and radical praise which will move heaven and still the enemy! Go with me as we take a look at the power of prayer, prophecy and praise in scripture, which is a threefold cord for victory in Jesus Name!

CHAPTER 1

WHY PRAYER, PROPHECY AND PRAISE?

"For though we walk in the flesh, we do not war after the flesh: (For the weapons of our warfare are not carnal, but mighty through God to the pulling down of strong holds." 2 Corinthians 10:3-4 KJV

Someone may be asking why write a book on prayer, prophecy and praise? Well the answer is simple. Prayer, prophecy and praise can found in just about every book of the Bible. All throughout the Bible these three powerful weapons of warfare have given Saints in the Old and New Testament the victory in the name of the LORD.

Think with me for a moment. All throughout the Bible we find someone praying, a prophecy being given and praise being lifted up to the LORD because of his great mercy, grace and victory given to the Saints! Prayer, prophecy and praise are a constant theme throughout the Bible and have enabled the people of God to overcome and get the victory in many areas of their lives.

As a student of the Bible and Pastor for many years, I can testify that prayer has been an important part of my walk with Christ since being born again in 1993. The majority of the ministries that I have sat under, or been a part of in my walk with the LORD have been prophetic in nature, and throughout my life I can honestly say that praise has stilled the avenger in times of trials and tribulation! (Psalm 8:2)

Before we begin, I would also like to give a disclaimer to all that are reading. I am by no means a subject matter expert on prayer, prophecy or praise, but I have personally received victory in many areas of my life, as a result of these Biblical principles, that the LORD has given to us.

There is also so much that we could cover as it relates to prayer, prophecy and praise. Due to the overwhelming amount of scriptures and stories in the Bible, it would be impossible to cover all of them! But we will discuss as many as possible.

I would like to start off by sharing a personal testimony about the power of prayer and prophecy. My first experience as it relates to the power of prayer and prophecy go back to December 1993 when I first got saved. While in the Navy stationed in Puerto Rico from 1990-1993, I began to fellowship with a few Navy brothers who were Muslims. At that time I was going through some personal trials, and the encouragement they provided was something I needed at that time. I grew up in church when I was young, but because of sin and the attitude that I had about church, it was not an option for me.

After a time of fellowship, I began to pray with these brothers and they gave me material about Islam and

Muslim prayers. I also began to pray with them and began praying five times a day. Our fellowship continued for about a year.

This was something my wife did not agree with. One day my wife and I had a big argument and disagreement. She challenged me to read the Bible in which I declined. I said over the past year I have gained so much wisdom and knowledge with these brothers. She then said, "If you want true wisdom, knowledge and understanding you should read the Bible." She then challenged me to read the book of Proverbs, the book of wisdom. She said, "If you are looking for true wisdom, read the Proverbs which is full of wisdom, and pray that God give you wisdom!" In order to stop the discord and division in our home, I told my wife that I would read the book of Proverbs, but that is all that I would read.

While reading Proverbs and seeking the LORD, I can recall a dear Sister who was a believer came by to see my wife and I one day. As we began to talk she said, "Jamal, I was in prayer and the LORD wanted me to give you a word of wisdom." I said, "Ok, what is it?" She said, "The LORD said you are looking for the right thing, but you are looking in the wrong place!"

I said, "Is that right? So what is the right thing?" She said God will reveal it in due season, but what you are doing is not the will of God for your life." I said ok, but until then, I am going to continue believing what I believe! My wife was totally upset with me because

I was so rude with my neighbor, but little did I know that God's prophetic Word would come to pass just as my neighbor told me!

Over the next few months I continued reading Proverbs, and I found that it was truly a book of wisdom. It had everything in it that pertains to life, godliness, speaking the right words, money, friends, decisions, making the right choices, and so much more. Then one day while reading Proverbs, I came across three verses of scripture that changed my life. I want to share those passages of scripture with you. They were Proverbs 3: 5-6, Proverbs 14:12 and Proverbs 16:25. Let's read!

"Trust in the LORD with all your heart, and lean not on your own understanding; in all your ways acknowledge Him, and He shall direct your paths."
Proverbs 3:5-6 NKJV

"There is a way that seems right to a man, but its end is the way of death."
Proverbs 14:12 NKJV

"There is a way that seems right to a man, but its end is the way of death."
Proverbs 16:25 NKJV

After reading these scriptures in Proverbs, my life was never the same. I just kept hearing this word in my head, "There is a way that seems right to a man, but its end is the way of death." The LORD began to deal with me concerning my life and all the things I held in my heart to be true. He also began to deal with me concerning all the wrong decisions I had made over the years. As a result, I began to pray and ask the LORD, "What do you want me to do? What decision should I make, and what steps should I take?"

While seeking and waiting on the LORD, these passages of scripture revealed to me how important it is to trust God with all your heart, and to lean not to your own understanding, but in all your ways acknowledge him and he will direct your paths.

The LORD also revealed to me that an individual can be doing something with all their heart, and believe it to be true and could be out of the will of God.

This is the mistake that many people make today. They believe something that is popular in the world, and it could be something they firmly believe in their heart to be true, but in the end it will lead to death.

Think about this for a moment. What if you were traveling on a long highway (without google maps) thinking that you are going in the right direction, and all of a sudden you realize you are going in the wrong direction headed toward the end of a cliff?

This is exactly what the scripture is saying, "There is a way that seems right to a man, woman, young man or young woman, but in the end it will lead to death.

In other words, it looks good now, it feels good now, it may be popular now, but what is the end result?

This is exactly what will happen to many people in the world today. They will live their life without wisdom, knowledge and understanding that comes from the LORD. In the end they will find that it is a way that leads to death. This was the dilemma that I was facing. God had revealed to me that he had another plan for my life, and it was not the one that I had chosen for myself.

After reading those scriptures, I couldn't sleep at night. A few weeks later I can remember waking up at 3am on a Saturday morning in December 1993, and fell on my knees in prayer. I cried out to God and said, "God, I want to know you as the one true God, please come into my heart. Jesus, if you are LORD, please save me. I want to know you, and I will serve you all the days of my life. I repent of my sins, and renounce anything that does not line up with your Word."

After I prayed this prayer, I felt the presence of God all over me. It was not an emotion or feeling. It was the Holy Spirit. I could remember praying many times before, but I never felt this powerful presence, and I began to weep. My wife woke up and said, "What is the matter?" I said, "I believe that the LORD has answered my prayer, and now I know what I must do." I felt a peace and freedom like never before as I went back to sleep.

I woke up the next morning and knew deep down that my prayers had been answered. As a result, I went to church that Sunday with my wife. My wife was shocked because in the past I didn't want to go to church. After a powerful message that was preached, they had an altar call and I publicly gave my life to Jesus Christ according to Romans 10:8-10, and to this day I have served the LORD with love, obedience faithfulness and joy!

I can still remember the prophetic word that my neighbor gave me in Puerto Rico, when she said, "The LORD said, "You are looking for the right thing, but looking in the wrong place, and he will reveal it in due season." I can honestly say that prayer and the prophetic word brought me to the place where I am today as a Pastor preaching and teaching the Word of God.

One thing I have found is that God always confirms his Word. The Bible says that God confirms his word by two or three witnesses.

"But if he will not hear thee, then take with thee one or two more, that in the mouth of two or three witnesses every word may be established."
Matthew 18:16 KJV

"This is the third time I am coming to you. In the mouth of two or three witnesses shall every word be established."
2 Corinthians 13:1 KJV

The prophetic word spoken to me in December 1993 was confirmed in June 1995, when my family and I were stationed in London, England. We were visiting a church where they were having a church conference, and there were well over 500 people in attendance. There was a Man of God from Florida, who was ministering, and the people were praising and worshipping the LORD, and the presence of God was powerful in the sanctuary!

All of sudden the preacher began to speak by the Holy Spirit and declare the Word of God. He then began to prophesy to a few people in the audience. He then pointed to me and began to prophesy saying:

Young man, "I don't know who you are, but there is a call on your life and you will be an ambassador for Christ. You will preach the Gospel and you will do great exploits in the name of the LORD!"

To be honest, I thought the man was crazy! I had just got saved and didn't know much about prophecy, but this man began to prophesy over my life and guess what? This prophecy was surely from the LORD.

Many years after that encounter, the LORD began to mature me and use me in many areas of ministry while serving in churches where I was assigned. The LORD also used me while I was in the military, and I had the opportunity to volunteer and serve in the Chapel, assisting with Bible studies, leading youth ministries, choirs, and other volunteer work.

I have also been preaching and teaching the gospel for over 22 years as of the writing of this book. Everything that was prophesied over my life has come to pass just as it was spoken by the Word of the LORD!

I share these awesome testimonies to show you that prayer and prophecy are very much a part of the Christian experience, and truth be told every believer should understand the importance of praise! If you truly believe that God is able to make all grace abound toward you, you must recognize that prayer is very important to your spiritual growth and life in Christ. Prophecy is also important to the body of Christ as well, because it encourages, edifies and comforts us. Prophecy also prepares us and warns us of things yet to come. Jesus even said in Matt 10:41, "He that receives a prophet in the name of a prophet shall receive a prophet's reward."

Praise is also a powerful spiritual weapon because it gives us the opportunity to exclaim the greatness of God, and to magnify, glorify and lift up the name of Jesus, who is worthy of all honor, glory, praise, dominion and majesty!

I am sure that I could get two or three witnesses as well that can testify that the power of prayer, prophecy and praise has blessed their lives, and given them the victory through healing, breakthrough, blessing, deliverance, protection and provision.

Even the Apostle Paul speaking about spiritual warfare and the armor of God ends by saying the following about prayer in Ephesians 6 verse 18:

"Praying always with all prayer and supplication in the Spirit, and watching thereunto with all perseverance and supplication for all saints."
Ephesians 6:18 KJV

We also find God using men and woman of God to edify, encourage, exhort and comfort his people through the prophetic word.

"But he that prophesies speaks unto men to edification, and exhortation, and comfort."
1 Corinthians 14:3 KJV

Last but not least, we find that the power of praise is a continual theme throughout the Bible. King David, one of Israel's most beloved Kings was radical as it relates to praise and worship. Many of the Psalms that he wrote expressed his pain, trust, love, thanksgiving, gratitude and praise to the LORD.

"I will be glad and rejoice in you; I will sing praise to your name, O Most High."
Psalms 9:2 NKJV

One of most well known scriptures on praise is found in Psalm 34: 1-3 NKJV

1 I will bless the LORD at all times; His praise shall continually be in my mouth.
2 My soul shall make its boast in the LORD; the

humble shall hear of it and be glad.
3 Oh, magnify the LORD with me, And let us exalt
His name together.

This psalm of praise speaks volumes because David is
saying that no matter what I go through, whether it
be good times, bad times, sad times, sickness times,
or people hating on me times! His praise shall
continually be in my mouth!

We also find that in the Bible there are over twenty
out of sixty six books that speak about a prophet, or
deal with prophets and prophecy. So in essence, the
Bible itself is prophetic! We must admit that most
people have no problem with prayer or praise, but
prophecy is another thing.

Some people don't really like to talk much about
prophecy, but prophecy is all throughout the Bible,
and is part of the Bible. Consider this; there are about
eighteen books in the Bible named after the Prophets
of God. Jesus was a prophet (Mark 6: 4), Moses was a
prophet (Deut 18: 15-18), the Bible even called
Abraham a prophet. (Gen 20: 7-9). Some of the most
important books of the Bible are from the prophets
Isaiah, Jeremiah, Ezekiel and Daniel.

What is amazing is that some people believe that
prophecy is complete after the resurrection of Christ
in what is referred to as cessation. In Christianity,
cessation is the doctrine that spiritual gifts such as

speaking in tongues, prophecy and healing ceased with the apostolic age.

If Jesus Christ is the same yesterday, today and forever more, why would there be a cessation of spiritual gifts? Even the Apostle Paul spoke about prophecy and prophets in the New Testament.

The book of Revelation is full of prophecies about the end times, and Jesus himself said that in the last days, false prophets would arise.

"Then many false prophets will rise up and deceive many."
Matthew 24:11 NKJV

"For false christs and false prophets will rise and show great signs and wonders to deceive, if possible, even the elect."
Matthew 24:24 NKJV

Are we not in the last days, with many false prophets arising and declaring false prophetic utterances? Declaring monetary prophecies and material things is not so prophetic to be truthful. True prophetic utterances will confirm all that is written in the Word of God, and will line up with the Word of God, as we near the second coming of the LORD Jesus Christ.

True prophetic utterances will speak truth to power as the true prophets of the Old Covenant did. Authentic prophets will flow in the prophetic like the anointed prophets Isaiah, Jeremiah, Ezekiel, Daniel, Elijah, and Samuel.

They will proclaim and confirm all that is in the LORD's heart concerning Israel, the church, and end time prophecy as the Apostles did. It will never be about them, it will always be about the true and living God, and all that he has predestined, purposed, planned, promised and prophesied in his Word.

The amazing thing that we should understand is if there are false prophets in the last days, then there shall also be authentic prophets in the last days as well. This makes perfect sense! All throughout the Bible we find prophecies being spoken, even in the first book of the Bible; Genesis.

In the first book of the Bible, we find the first prophecy by our Heavenly Father to Adam, Eve and the serpent after they sinned in the Garden of Eden. Let's read!

Genesis 3:14-16 NKJV
14 So the LORD God said to the serpent: "Because you have done this, you are cursed more than all cattle, And more than every beast of the field; On your belly you shall go, and you shall eat dust All the days of your life.
15 And I will put enmity between you and the woman, and between your seed and her Seed; He shall bruise your head, And you shall bruise His heel."
16 To the woman He said: "I will greatly multiply

your sorrow and your conception; In pain you shall bring forth children; Your desire shall be for your husband, And he shall rule over you."

We find that the last book of the Bible; Revelation is prophetic as well.

Revelation 1:1-3 NKJV
1 The Revelation of Jesus Christ, which God gave Him to show His servants--things which must shortly take place, and He sent and signified it by His angel to His servant John,
2 who bore witness to the word of God, and to the testimony of Jesus Christ, to all things that he saw.
3 Blessed is he who reads and those who hear the words of this prophecy, and keep those things which are written in it; for the time is near.

A blessing is even released over the one who reads, hears, and keeps the words of the prophecy that are written in the book of Revelation!

So regardless of the dispensation that we are in, prophecy in the New Covenant is just as important now, as it was in the Old Covenant.

The Bible says in Roman 15: 4, "That whatsoever things were written before were written for our learning, that we through the patience and comfort of the Scriptures might have hope."
Romans 15:4 NKJV

So although we are a New Testament church we need to understand the profound principles of prayer, prophecy and praise are Biblical, and will transform your life when you believe and embrace them.

As it relates to prayer, how many of us know that in the last days that we live in, God requires us to pray in order to achieve his Kingdom agenda? In light of all the events that are happening in the earth, we should be praying now more than ever before.

Consider the scripture of Luke 21: 25-28 NKJV

25 "And there will be signs in the sun, in the moon, and in the stars; and on the earth distress of nations, with perplexity, the sea and the waves roaring;
26 men's hearts failing them from fear and the expectation of those things which are coming on the earth, for the powers of the heavens will be shaken.
27 Then they will see the Son of Man coming in a cloud with power and great glory.
28 Now when these things begin to happen, look up and lift up your heads, because your redemption draws near."

I mean over the years we have witnessed an increase in eclipses, pestilences, hurricanes, tornados, tsunamis, floods, fires out of control, wars and rumors of wars. These are signs of the times!

When you read Luke 21, Jesus is prophesying about the end times, and gives us some profound prophetic wisdom as it relates to watching and praying in verse 36.

"Watch therefore, and pray always that you may be counted worthy to escape all these things that will come to pass, and to stand before the Son of Man."

Luke 21:36 NKJV

The LORD himself said that we should watch and pray that we would be counted worthy to escape all these things that will come to pass! Is anyone watching and praying?

When we read the scriptures we will find that there is nothing that God does in the earth without the use of a man or woman. In the beginning God created the heavens and the earth, but he created a man and woman to maintain it.

"The heaven, even the heavens are the LORD's; but the earth He has given to the children of men." Psalms 115:16 NKJV

So when you pray and come into divine alignment with his will, you are partnering with God to achieve his Kingdom purposes in the earth. The greatest words that anyone could ever pray are "Lord may your perfect will be done in my life" and "Not my will but your will be done!" Now understand there are some people that have not gotten to that place yet, because their will is still in control.

As long as your will is in control, God's will cannot be done! It's either your will or his will! You cannot do God's will and your will at the same time. The problem we have with many believers today is that they have not completely surrendered their will to the LORD!

Why do we need to pray?

One of the most profound reasons for us to pray is that God desires to hear from heaven, forgive our sin and heal our land.

In the book of 2 Chronicles 7, the LORD is speaking to Solomon, the Son of David who has just completed the building of the Temple of God. Let's read!

2 Chronicles 7:11-14 KJV
11 Thus Solomon finished the house of the LORD, and the king's house: and all that came into Solomon's heart to make in the house of the LORD, and in his own house, he prosperously effected.
12 And the LORD appeared to Solomon by night, and said unto him, I have heard thy prayer, and have chosen this place to myself for a house of sacrifice.
13 If I shut up heaven that there be no rain, or if I command the locusts to devour the land, or if I send pestilence among my people;
14 If my people, which are called by my name, shall humble themselves, and pray, and seek my face, and turn from their wicked ways; then will I hear from heaven, and will forgive their sin, and will heal their land.

Notice that there are four conditions that the LORD gave to Solomon in verse 14 which were profound in the days of Solomon, and even so much more today!

1. If my people who are called by my name.
2. Humble themselves and pray.
3. Seek my face.
4. Turn from their wicked ways.

The LORD said, "Then will I hear from heaven, and will forgive their sin, and heal their land." Notice that the condition of healing and restoration starts with prayer. This is why it is so important that every believer have a consistent prayer life!

Jesus praying in the Garden of Gethsemane

One of the most profound examples of praying and seeking the Fathers will through prayer can be found in the Garden of Gethsemane, as Jesus was preparing to go the cross, to die for the sins of the world. It is one of the most profound prayers found in the New Testament and is an excellent example of prayer, humility, and obedience to our Heavenly Father. Let's read!

Matthew 26:36-46 NKJV
36 Then Jesus came with them to a place called Gethsemane, and said to the disciples, "Sit here while I go and pray over there."
37 And He took with Him Peter and the two sons of Zebedee, and He began to be sorrowful and deeply distressed.
38 Then He said to them, "My soul is exceedingly sorrowful, even to death. Stay here and watch with me."
39 He went a little farther and fell on His face, and prayed, saying, "O My Father, if it is possible, let this cup pass from me; nevertheless, not as I will, but as you will."
40 Then He came to the disciples and found them sleeping, and said to Peter, "What! Could you not watch with me one hour?
41 Watch and pray, lest you enter into temptation.

The spirit indeed is willing, but the flesh is weak."
42 Again, a second time, He went away and prayed, saying, "O My Father, if this cup cannot pass away from me unless I drink it, your will be done."
43 And He came and found them asleep again, for their eyes were heavy.
44 So He left them, went away again, and prayed the third time, saying the same words.
45 Then He came to His disciples and said to them, "Are you still sleeping and resting? Behold, the hour is at hand, and the Son of Man is being betrayed into the hands of sinners.
46 Rise let us be going. See, My betrayer is at hand."

We find in Matthew chapter 26 that although Jesus was the Son of God, he understood the power of prayer as it relates to the Fathers will. Yet during the time that he needed the disciples most, they were spiritually and physically asleep and couldn't pray!

Isn't this amazing? There is so much revelation in these passages of scripture. Even Jesus Christ understood that prayer is important as it relates to doing the will of the Father! Anytime that we do anything as it relates to the Kingdom of God, we must pray for wisdom, guidance, direction, protection and come into agreement with the perfect will of our Father in Heaven.

Let's take a look at this scenario in the Garden of Gethsemane. Jesus knew that he would be going to the cross soon and is now praying to the Father for strength, and needed the disciples to intercede for him. The Bible says in Matt 26:37-38, that he took Peter, James and John with him to pray and he was exceedingly sorrowful even to death! He then said to them, "Stay here and watch with me."

"And He took with Him Peter and the two sons of Zebedee, and He began to be sorrowful and deeply distressed. Then He said to them, "My soul is exceedingly sorrowful, even to death. Stay here and watch with me."
Matthew 26:37-38 NKJV

Jesus understood that what he was about to go through at the cross was important and significant and he needed supernatural strength. He was about to take the sins of the world on himself, and he felt the weight of it all coming down on him. The cross, the sin of the people, betrayal, pain, and death was about to come to pass.

Think about this for a moment, if you were about to do something that was totally life changing, significant, and affected the lives of many people, there would be some anxiety and fear of the unknown.

This is what Jesus was going through, and he needed the disciples to cover him in prayer to lighten the load, with the sorrow and heaviness that was on his heart!

When you read the account of Jesus in the Garden of Gethsemane, you can see the urgency that Jesus is displaying as it relates to prayer. Not only is he praying, but he requested that the disciples; Peter, James and John pray with him. The Bible says that as he prayed, he came to the disciples and they were sleeping. As a result Jesus rebuked them saying, "Could you not pray with me for one hour?"

Isn't this a profound statement? Because many churches in the Body of Christ often struggle with leaders and members, who don't understand the importance of prayer. It is amazing that we have so much time for everything else, such as movies and so many other pleasures, yet the hour of prayer can be a struggle for many people.

I want to warn you that a prayerless Christian is a powerless Christian. If you don't have a desire to pray, you could very well become the prey. If you are a leader or member of a church, the most important thing that you can do as a member of that local community of Christ is to pray for your leadership and pray for one another.

If you are a person that does not enjoy prayer, your flesh is weak. Why do I say this? Because Jesus said in Matt 26: 4, "Watch and pray, lest you enter into temptation. The spirit indeed is willing, but the flesh is weak."

The spirit of a man or woman is always ready to engage in prayer, and to do spiritual things that bring glory to God. The flesh is the opposite. It does not like to pray, it does not like to fast, and it does not like to study the Word. Yet, the pleasurable things of the world excite the flesh.

The Bible says that as Jesus prayed, he found them sleeping three times. After this encounter, Judas and the temple guards arrested Jesus.

Matthew 26:43-46 NKJV
43 And He came and found them asleep again, for their eyes were heavy.
44 So He left them, went away again, and prayed the third time, saying the same words.
45 Then He came to His disciples and said to them, "Are you still sleeping and resting? Behold, the hour is at hand, and the Son of Man is being betrayed into the hands of sinners.
46 Rise let us be going. See, My betrayer is at hand."

We all know that this prophecy had to come to pass because Jesus had a mission, and it was to go to the cross to fulfill prophecy. But despite prophecy being fulfilled, we cannot miss this teachable aspect of standing strong in prayer for one another, especially our leaders.

We need to understand that prayer is the key to victory, and it starts with covering our leaders, churches, families and one another. When we engage in persistent, powerful prayer, we get the victory. When we are asleep and don't engage the enemy through prayer, we are certain to be defeated!

Moses and Israel get the victory

A great example of intercession, prayer and standing in the gap for leaders, is when Moses and the children of Israel battled the enemy Amalek in Exodus 17: 8-13. Let's read!

8 Now Amalek came and fought with Israel in Rephidim.
9 And Moses said to Joshua, "Choose us some men and go out, fight with Amalek. Tomorrow I will stand on the top of the hill with the rod of God in my hand."
10 So Joshua did as Moses said to him, and fought with Amalek. And Moses, Aaron, and Hurl went up to the top of the hill.
11 And so it was, when Moses held up his hand, that Israel prevailed; and when he let down his hand, Amalek prevailed.
12 But Moses' hands became heavy; so they took a stone and put it under him, and he sat on it. And Aaron and Hur supported his hands, one on one side, and the other on the other side; and his hands were steady until the going down of the sun.
13 So Joshua defeated Amalek and his people with the edge of the sword.

In this passage of scripture we see a wonderful picture of intercession and prayer. As Moses and Israel battle the enemy, Moses holds up the rod which was a symbol of God's power with him!

The Bible says that when he held up his hands that Israel prevailed. When he let down his hands, the enemy prevailed. Now don't miss the revelation in this passage of scripture. When Moses held up his hands, which is symbolic of lifting your hands in prayer or praise to the Most High God they prevailed! When his hands got heavy, he dropped them and the enemy prevailed!

So what did those anointed leaders and servants do? Aaron and Hur got on the left and right hand side of Moses and lifted up his hands so that they were held high! Not only that, but they took a stone, sat it under him and held his hands high until Israel who was led by Joshua got complete victory over the enemy. Notice that they held both of Moses hands high to the LORD and got complete victory. The most powerful indicator of praise and prayer is when we lift our hands high to the LORD!

What can we learn from this?
1. We must keep our hands lifted to God in prayer and praise to get the victory.
2. We need anointed leaders and servants that will hold up leadership arms in the midst of the battle.
3. We need the support of leaders in prayer to get absolute victory.
4. Victory is certain when leaders are surrounded by prayer warriors and intercessors who will ensure that leaders are not weary, covered in prayer and stand by their side in the midst of the battle.

CHAPTER 2

THE POWER OF PRAYER IN SCRIPTURE

"And he spoke a parable unto them to this end, that men ought always to pray, and not to faint."
Luke 18:1 KJV

When we look at scripture we find that Jesus Christ provides one of the most profound examples of one who was always in prayer. Although Jesus was the Son of God, he was also the Son of Man while he was in the earth realm, and was subject to natural circumstances just as we were.

What is amazing to me is that we find him praying constantly in the Gospels. Now let me pause for a moment. If Jesus the Son of God had to pray and stood on the Word of God, how much more should we?

The spiritual virtues that keep us strong spiritually are the Word of God and prayer. I don't believe that a person can be all that God called them to be if they are not a student of the Word and prayer! If we are going to be victorious in our walk with Christ, we must follow the example of Christ who prayed often! Let's look at some examples in scripture!

"When all the people were baptized, it came to pass that Jesus also was baptized; and while He prayed, the heaven was opened."
Luke 3:21 NKJV

"So He Himself often withdrew into the wilderness and prayed."
Luke 5:16 NKJV

"Now it came to pass in those days that He went out to the mountain to pray, and continued all night in prayer to God."
Luke 6:12 NKJV

Did you get that? Jesus continued all night in prayer!

"Then He took the five loaves and the two fish, and looking up to heaven, He blessed and broke them, and gave them to the disciples to set before the multitude."
Luke 9:16 NKJV

Jesus even prayed and blessed God before eating food!

Luke 9:28-31 NKJV
28 Now it came to pass, about eight days after these sayings, that He took Peter, John, and James and went up on the mountain to pray.
29 As He prayed, the appearance of His face was altered, and His robe became white and glistening.
30 And behold, two men talked with Him, who were Moses and Elijah,
31 who appeared in glory and spoke of His decease which He was about to accomplish at Jerusalem.

As you can see Jesus was always in prayer. One of the most profound scriptures concerning prayer is when the disciples saw Jesus in prayer and asked him to teach them how to pray.

"Now it came to pass, as He was praying in a certain place, when He ceased, that one of His disciples said to Him, "Lord, teach us to pray, as John also taught his disciples."
Luke 11:1 NKJV

Isn't it amazing that the disciples saw Jesus casting out demons, performing miracles, healing the sick, and raising the dead, yet they asked, "Lord teach us how to pray, as John also taught his disciples." So we see that prayer can be taught!

There is no reason why any believer that names the name of Jesus Christ should be afraid to pray! There are prayer principles in the word that will enable every believer to be successful in prayer.

Jesus response to the disciples request to teach them to pray was a simple powerful prayer which is the Lord's Prayer! Let's read!

"And he said unto them, when you pray say, "Our Father which art in heaven, hallowed be thy name. Thy kingdom come. Thy will be done, as in heaven, so in earth. Give us day by day our daily bread. And forgive us our sins; for we also forgive every one that is indebted to us. And lead us not into temptation; but deliver us from evil."
Luke 11:2-4 KJV

As we see from the scriptures, Jesus taught them a simple prayer which can be prayed on a regular basis. We also see from the scriptures that prayer can be taught. In other words there are principles that relate to prayer that anyone who does not know how to pray

can learn. Just remember that some things are taught and some things are caught!
What does that mean? There are some things that you can be taught by others, but there are some things you have to catch by the Holy Spirit who will teach you!

Someone may be reading this and saying the Lord's Prayer is so simple. Yes it is simple, but it is the prayer that was given to us by Jesus Christ. It contains everything we need as it relates to coming into agreement with heavens Kingdom plan, fulfilling the will of God, and getting our needs supplied.

What is interesting is that the disciples asked Jesus to teach them to pray as John taught his disciples. (Luke 11:1) There is a simple formula that can help anyone to pray with confidence and power. That prayer is called the ACTS of PRAYER. This is something that is not new. Many believers' young and old have used it and still use it today.

These are basic elements that should be included in our prayers and they are Adoration, Confession, Thanksgiving, and Supplication or "ACTS" for short.

A – Adoration means to adore God. It is to worship and praise Him, to honor and exalt Him with all of our heart, soul, mind and strength! Adoration demonstrates our reverence, awe, love, and gratitude. This is why we say, "Our Father which is in heaven hallowed be your holy Name! (Psalm 96:9, John 4:24, Luke 11: 2)

C – Confession gives us the opportunity to reveal any sin in our life that needs to be confessed. By seeing God in purity, holiness, and love, we become aware of our own sinfulness and unworthiness. Confessing our sin and receiving His forgiveness restores our fellowship, and clears the channel for God to hear and answer our prayers. We should also forgive and release others as pray as well. Jesus always connected the answering of our prayers to forgiving others. (Prov 28:13, Matt 6:14-15, 1 John 1:8-9, Luke 11:4).

T – Thanksgiving gives us a consistent opportunity to express our praise and thanks to God for his goodness, grace, mercy and supplying our needs. God's Word commands us, "Give thanks in all circumstances" because this is God's will for you in Christ Jesus." The Bible also says we should enter into His gates with thanksgiving, and into His courts with praise. Be thankful to Him, and bless His name. (Psalm 100:4, Psalm 107:1, 1 Thessalonians 5:18).

S – Supplication includes our petitions, requests, needs and intercession for others. As you pray to the LORD be sensitive to the Holy Spirit. Pray about your problems, pray for wisdom and guidance, pray for strength to resist temptation, pray for comfort in time of sorrow, pray for others, pray for your family, your children, your parents, neighbors, friends, community, city and country. Pray for your pastor and missionaries, pray for leaders to whom God has given special responsibility, and above all pray for those in authority over you. (Matt 7: 7-8, Luke 11: 9-13, 1 Timothy 2:1-5)

All throughout scripture we are exhorted to pray! Jesus told us in Luke 18: 1, "Men ought always to pray and not to faint." Paul told us in 1 Thess 5: 17, "Pray without ceasing." He also told us in Eph 6:18, "To pray always with all prayer and supplication in the Spirit, being watchful to this end with all perseverance and supplication for all the saints."

Praying and Speaking to Mountains

In the book of Mark chapter 11, the LORD Jesus gives the disciples additional instruction on the power of prayer. As they were journeying from Bethany, the Bible says that Jesus was hungry and decided to pick figs from a tree and found none. He then cursed the fig tree in the presence of the disciples as they continued on. Let's read! (There is a prayer lesson in this story that we will see in a moment.)

Mark 11:12-14 NKJV
12 Now the next day, when they had come out from Bethany, He was hungry.
13 And seeing from afar a fig tree having leaves, He went to see if perhaps He would find something on it. When He came to it, He found nothing but leaves, for it was not the season for figs.
14 In response Jesus said to it, "Let no one eat fruit from you ever again." And His disciples heard it.

As Jesus and the disciples continued on their way, they went to Jerusalem and entered the temple, and Jesus saw that they were doing everything except praying and worshipping. Jesus respond is profound. Let's read!

Mark 11:15-17 KJV
15 And they come to Jerusalem: and Jesus went into the temple, and began to cast out them that sold and bought in the temple, and overthrew the tables of the moneychangers, and the seats of them that sold doves;
16 And would not suffer that any man should carry any vessel through the temple.
17 And he taught, saying unto them, is it not written, my house shall be called of all nations the house of prayer? But ye have made it a den of thieves.

Jesus was so upset at the people in the temple that he began to turn over their tables, and throw them out of the temple. The Gospel of John records that he made a whip and began to beat them.

"When He had made a whip of cords, He drove them all out of the temple, with the sheep and the oxen, and poured out the changers' money and overturned the tables."
John 2:15 NKJV

Jesus saw that they were doing more buying and selling then they were praying and worshipping in the temple. Jesus said, "Is it not written, "My house shall be called a house of prayer? But you have made it a den of thieves."

In other words, the house of God is place of prayer and worship. So the question is why do we allow any and everything to go on in houses of worship? Yes we are the church and it is a building, but it is building with God's name on it! We must be careful to not allow the house of God to become a place of merchandise where we allow any and everything to go on besides prayer and worship!

As they returned from their journey and passed the fig tree, Peter remembered that Jesus cursed the fig tree. He was amazed that it was dried up at the roots.

Mark 11:20-21 NKJV
20 Now in the morning, as they passed by, they saw the fig tree dried up from the roots.
21 And Peter, remembering, said to Him, "Rabbi, look! The fig tree which you cursed has withered away."

Jesus was so wise that he used this opportunity to give them a lesson on faith and prayer.

Mark 11:22-23 NKJV
22 So Jesus answered and said to them, "Have faith in God.
23 For assuredly, I say to you, whosoever says to this mountain, 'Be removed and be cast into the sea,' and does not doubt in his heart, but believes that those things he says will be done, he will have whatever he says.

Jesus told the disciples if they have faith in God, and used that faith to speak or say to the mountain, which is representative of situations, circumstances, and issues that are before them to be removed and cast into the sea; they would receive whatever they said. Then he gives them the prayer revelation.

Mark 11:24-26 NKJV
24 Therefore I say to you, whatever things you ask when you pray, believe that you receive them, and you will have them.
25 And whenever you stand praying, if you have anything against anyone, forgive him, that your Father in heaven may also forgive you, your trespasses.
26 But if you do not forgive, neither will your Father in heaven forgive your trespasses."

In other words Jesus was saying that if you have a little faith in God, and do not doubt in your heart, but believe that those things you speak, say, and pray will come to pass, you will receive it! In Matthew 17:20, there is a similar account, but Matthew says, if you have faith the size of a mustard seed!

"So Jesus said to them, "Because of your unbelief; for assuredly, I say to you, if you have faith as a mustard seed, you will say to this mountain, 'Move from here to there,' and it will move; and nothing will be impossible for you."
Matthew 17:20 NKJV

Last but not least, we notice in scripture that Jesus always connects our forgiveness to answered prayer. If you desire to receive answered prayer from the LORD, we must have a clean heart that is free from anger, bitterness, resentment and malice.

Praying in the Spirit

Sometimes we know what mountains are before us and sometimes we just don't what to pray for. There have been times in my life where I knew exactly what to pray for, and other times, I just needed to cry out to the LORD. The Apostle Paul said something very profound in Romans chapter 8. Let's read!

Romans 8:26-27 NKJV
26 Likewise the Spirit also helps in our weaknesses. For we do not know what we should pray for as we ought, but the Spirit Himself makes intercession for us with groanings which cannot be uttered.
27 Now He who searches the hearts knows what the mind of the Spirit is, because He makes intercession for the saints according to the will of God.

Paul is saying that the Holy Spirit helps us in our weaknesses. Sometimes we just don't know what to pray for, but the Spirit of Truth knows all things and will help us to pray. There will be times in life where we may be dealing with a situation that may be too much for us, and Paul says that the Holy Spirit will intercede for us.

Many of us know this as praying in the spirit. I don't know about you, but I have experienced some trials and tribulations in my life where I needed the help of the Holy Spirit, because I just didn't know what to pray for! The Comforter searches our hearts and knows exactly what we are going through and what we need. The Bible says that he makes intercession for us according to the will of God.

This is good news for us. Because there are some things we know what to pray for, and other things that God himself will give us the wisdom, comfort, strength and grace we need to get through, or overcome a situation in our lives. Why is it important to pray in the spirit?

Listen to what the Bible says about the Holy Spirit.

John 14:26 – "But the Helper, the Holy Spirit, whom the Father will send in My name, He will teach you all things, and bring to your remembrance all things that I said to you."

John 15:26 – "But when the Comforter is come, whom I will send unto you from the Father, even the Spirit of truth, which proceeds from the Father, he shall testify of me."

John 16:13 – "However, when He, the Spirit of truth, has come, He will guide you into all truth; for He will not speak on His own authority, but whatever He hears He will speak; and He will tell you things to come."

John 16:14 – "He will glorify me, for He will take of what is Mine and declare it to you."

John 16:15 – "All things that the Father has are mine. Therefore I said that He will take of mine and declare it to you."

As we can see, the Holy Spirit knows all things and will reveal all things to us as we pray in the spirit, and allow him to intercede for us.

James Exhortation and Wisdom to Pray

One of the most powerful exhortations to pray can be found in James chapter 5, verses 13-18, we learn some powerful principles of prayer by the Apostle James. James mentions prayer at least seven times in six verses of scripture.

James 5:13-18 NKJV

13 Is anyone among you suffering? Let him pray. Is anyone cheerful? Let him sing psalms.

14 Is anyone among you sick? Let him call for the elders of the church, and let them pray over him, anointing him with oil in the name of the Lord.

15 And the prayer of faith will save the sick, and the Lord will raise him up. And if he has committed sins, he will be forgiven.

16 Confess your trespasses to one another, and pray for one another, that you may be healed. The effective, fervent prayer of a righteous man avails much.

17 Elijah was a man with a nature like ours, and he prayed earnestly that it would not rain; and it did not rain on the land for three years and six months.

18 And he prayed again, and the heaven gave rain, and the earth produced its fruit.'

In these passages of scripture we find that no matter what you are going through, the answer to all things is prayer! What is so profound is that James mentions the mighty Prophet Elijah from the Old Testament who did great miracles in the name of the LORD. James said that although he was a powerful man of God, he had a human nature or was subject to passions like you and me.

Sometimes we forget that. Especially in the body of Christ, because although we are filled with the spirit and led by the spirit, we have a human nature and we are subject to passions, feelings and emotions.

Do you understand what James is saying though? That although Elijah was a mighty prophet of God and stopped the rain for three and a half years, (1 Kings 17:1), he was a human being like you and me! Let's read what James said:

Jas 5:17 Elijah was a man subject to passions like as we are, and he prayed earnestly that it would not rain; and it did not rain on the land for three years and six months.

Jas 5:18 And he prayed again, and the heaven gave rain, and the earth produced its fruit.

If you are not aware of how powerful Elijah the Prophet was, let me remind you of what he did in the name of the LORD! God used Elijah mightily to raise a boy from the dead, (1 Kings 17: 21) called down fire from heaven, (1 Kings 18: 37-38), killed four hundred and fifty false prophets by himself, (1 Kings 18:40) but yet he was a human being with a nature like you and me!

This should encourage someone that God is not a respecter of persons, and that he hears all the prayers of all his beloved and righteous children!

I want you to know that although you may not be a minister or clergy. It makes no difference! James is making the case that prayer is for everyone, and God hears the prayers of all his righteous saints!

Now understand that each and every one of us has emotions, passions, needs and desires. The only difference in being called to ministry is that God has anointed, sanctified, and set individuals aside for Kingdom purposes in the earth.

The Bible says in James 5:16, "Confess your faults one to another, and pray one for another, that you may be healed. **The effectual fervent prayer of a righteous man avails much."**

So today I want to encourage someone that prayer is important and that you should pray with power concerning every situation in your life. As a result God will open the windows of heaven and pour you out a blessing that you would not have room enough to receive! How do I know this to be true? Listen to Luke 11:9-12 NKJV:

9 So I say to you, ask, and it will be given to you; seek, and you will find; knock, and it will be opened to you.
10 For everyone who asks receive, and he who seeks finds, and to him who knocks it will be opened.
11 If a son asks for bread from any father among you, will he give him a stone? Or if he asks for a fish, will he give him a serpent instead of a fish?
12 Or if he asks for an egg, will he offer him a scorpion?

The key to praying in agreement with God is coming into agreement with those things that God has already purposed in the earth. God's will for us is revealed in his word. Some of the most powerful prayers to pray are the word of God. Yes, God hears our words, but if God honors his Word, wouldn't it be wise to pray that which he has said in his Word?

Now understand that God has ordained certain things in the heavens that man must partner with him to achieve his Kingdom purposes in the earth. God can and has the power to do all things, but he has chosen to use human beings as instruments of his righteousness in the earth.

My assignment in this book is to empower you and to show you the significance of prayer, prophecy and praise, and how important it is to embrace these Kingdom virtues as it relates to your relationship in Christ. Not only is that, but prayer, prophecy and praise are going to be a very important part of what God is doing in the last days!
Prayer, prophecy and praise are weapons of warfare for the believer. These weapons of our warfare are not carnal, fleshly, or human devices, but they are mighty in God.

"For though we walk in the flesh, we do not war after the flesh: (For the weapons of our warfare are not carnal, but mighty through God to the pulling down of strong holds."
2 Corinthians 10:3-4 KJV

In order to pull down strongholds in the spiritual realm that hinder our communities, cities, and country it will take prayer, prophecy and praise! In order to manifest all that God has purposed for us as it relates to the Kingdom plan of God it will take prayer, prophecy and praise.

Now each of these weapons in their own capacity are powerful, but together they are like spiritual dynamite!

Prayer, prophecy and praise are important for every member of the Body of Christ. Because when you pray, you are looking for the answer to that request, and the answer may come in many ways.

It may come through the Word of God, a prophetic word, a devotional, a book, a word of confirmation, or a sermon! And when the answer comes, there should be much praise to the Lord for answered prayer!

Moses the Prophet in Prayer

As you know Moses was given the assignment to bring the children of Israel into the Promised Land, and it was a monumental task. The people constantly complained, rebelled and questioned his leadership. They were disobedient and always murmuring and complaining! Unfortunately, this is how many believers are today. Yet, we find that these things only hinder our faith and relationship with the LORD. Look at Numbers 11: 1-3

Numbers 11:1-3 KJV
1 And when the people complained, it displeased the

LORD: and the LORD heard it; and his anger was kindled; and the fire of the LORD burnt among them, and consumed them that were in the uttermost parts of the camp.

2 And the people cried unto Moses, and when Moses prayed unto the LORD, the fire was quenched.

3 And he called the name of the place Taberah: because the fire of the LORD burnt among them.

Let me say something about this. There are always going to be people in the church that complain or have something to say about everything. The best thing to do is to pray and ask God to help, because the Holy Spirit will always lead you to pray, not complain and gossip.

Prayer can do far more than murmuring and complaining. It will do far more than gossip, and it will do far more than accusing and finger pointing at Gods appointed leader.

"And the people cried unto Moses; and when Moses prayed unto the LORD, the fire was quenched." Numbers 11:2 KJV

In Numbers chapter 11, verses 4-9, we find the people of God complaining to Moses about the miracle bread from heaven; manna. In response and frustration, Moses cries out to the LORD for help in Number 11:10-15.

Numbers 11:10-15 NKJV

10 Then Moses heard the people weeping throughout their families, everyone at the door of his tent; and the anger of the LORD was greatly aroused; Moses also was displeased.

11 So Moses said to the LORD, "Why have You afflicted Your servant? And why have I not found favor in Your sight, that You have laid the burden of all these people on me?

12 Did I conceive all these people? Did I beget them, that You should say to me, 'Carry them in your bosom, as a guardian carries a nursing child,' to the land which You swore to their fathers?

13 Where am I to get meat to give to all these people? For they weep all over me, saying, 'Give us meat that we may eat.'

14 I am not able to bear all these people alone, because the burden is too heavy for me.

15 If You treat me like this, please kill me here and now—if I have found favor in Your sight—and do not let me see my wretchedness!"

I would like to pause for a moment to talk about the ministry of Moses and the children of Israel. There are many people who may be reading this who are ministers and leaders in the ministry, who can certainly understand Moses frustration.

Moses is trying to do the will of God in bringing the people into the Promised Land, and the complaints, cries and frustration of the people are too much for him. You can see the frustration that is upon Moses because he is now complaining to the LORD about the people of God.

In verses 10-15, Moses is so upset that he is now arguing with God and saying, "Did I birth them? Are they my children? What am I going to do? LORD why are you putting this burden on me? As a matter of fact, "LORD just kill me and take me home." This is too much for me? Wow, this is certainly a lot of discouragement and pressure on the man of God! Anybody ever felt like that?

Despite all the pain Moses is feeling, God has a plan. We need to remember that God always has a plan. One thing I have learned to do as a leader in ministry is to pray and cry out to the LORD.

Let's be real, people can and will frustrate you, but the power of prayer is what we need to get supernatural and divine assistance from heaven.

I would also like to say something to anyone who may be a member of a church. The best thing that you can do when things may not be going well in your church is to pray. I have heard where churches have locked Pastor's out, cursed, fought in church and did everything except agree in prayer. Listen, murmuring, complaining, gossiping and lashing out at God's leadership is the worst thing that one can do. Prayer is what makes the difference!

In response to the people's complaints and Moses cries to the LORD, God gives Moses some profound instructions to appoint seventy Elders in whom he will take of the spirit that is on Moses, and put it on them to assist in the work of the ministry.

Numbers 11:16-17 KJV
16 And the LORD said unto Moses, Gather unto me seventy men of the elders of Israel, whom thou know to be the elders of the people, and officers over them; and bring them unto the tabernacle of the congregation, that they may stand there with thee. 17 And I will come down and talk with thee there: and I will take of the spirit which is upon thee, and will put it upon them; and they shall bear the burden of the people with thee, that thou bear it not thyself alone.

This story is powerful because although Moses is the unparalleled leader, he is not alone. God said that he would take of the spirit that is on Moses and put it on the seventy Elders. In other words the same spirit that empowers Moses will empower the Elders.

This is an amazing and profound story. It shows us that despite what we may experience in life or ministry, God has a plan and through the power of prayer, God will make a way, raise up, appoint, and assign men and woman of God to assist in the work of the ministry.

This is important because as we see with Moses, God understands the pressures of doing Kingdom work and ministry. As a result, he will assign people who have the same heart, mind and spirit as the visionary to assist in shepherding, and doing the work of the ministry. But as we see, it all starts with prayer!

CHAPTER 3

THE POWER OF PROPHECY IN SCRIPTURE

"Surely the Lord GOD will do nothing, but he reveals his secret unto his servants the prophets."
Amos 3:7 KJV

In the last chapter we looked at how powerful prayer is seen through the examples of Jesus Christ and Moses. There is so much more we could cover and we will in later chapters, but let's look at the power of prophecy in scripture. We will pick up in the Old Testament where we left off with Moses.

In the last chapter we looked at Numbers chapter 11 were the LORD gave Moses instructions to bring seventy Elders to the temple. The LORD said that he would meet them there, and take of the spirit that was on Moses and put it upon the seventy Elders. Let's read!

Numbers 11:24-25 KJV
24 And Moses went out, and told the people the words of the LORD, and gathered the seventy men of the elders of the people, and set them round about the tabernacle.
25 And the LORD came down in a cloud, and spoke unto him, and took of the spirit that was upon him, and gave it unto the seventy elders: and it came to pass, that, when the spirit rested upon them, they prophesied, and did not cease.

Now the question we need to ask is what kind of spirit was on Moses? Well when we look at the life of Moses, there were at least five virtues that Moses had, and they were:

1. The spirit of a shepherd.
2. The spirit of meekness.
3. The spirit of prayer.
4. The spirit of intercession.
5. The spirit of prophecy.

These are profound virtues that every leader that serves God's people should have.

As Moses gathered the seventy Elders as commanded by the LORD, the spirit of God fell on them and they prophesied!

Numbers 11:25 KJV
25 And the LORD came down in a cloud, and spoke unto him, and took of the spirit that was upon him, and gave it unto the seventy elders: and it came to pass, that, when the spirit rested upon them, they prophesied, and did not cease.

Isn't this amazing? This is my prayer in ministry! LORD, take of the spirit that is on me and put it on the leaders, and the members of the ministry! So that we all have the same spirit of agreement as it relates to the work of the ministry!

The Bible says in verse 25: "And the LORD came down in a cloud, and spoke unto him, and took of the spirit that was upon him, and gave it unto the seventy elders: and it came to pass, that when the spirit rested upon them, they prophesied, and did not cease."

Now let's analyze this for a moment. The LORD said that he would take of the spirit that was on Moses and put it on the seventy Elders.

As Moses and the seventy Elders gathered together, the spirit of God fell upon them and they prophesied! This was a sign that the prophetic spirit that was on Moses to carry the load, and shepherd God's people was also on them.

We mentioned earlier that there were certain attributes that were on the man of God that were put upon the seventy Elders. It's interesting to note that Moses was a shepherd, he was meek, he interceded, and he prayed. God could have placed any of these virtues upon the seventy Elders, but he placed on them the spirit of prophecy! Let's talk about this for a moment because the Bible says that Moses was a prophet in Deuteronomy 34:10.

"But since then there has not arisen in Israel a prophet like Moses, whom the LORD knew face to face."
Deuteronomy 34:10 NKJV

What is even more amazing is when the LORD took of the spirit that was on Moses and put it on seventy Elders; there were two other individuals that received of the spirit as well.

Numbers 11:26-29 NKJV
26 But two men had remained in the camp: the name of one was Eldad, and the name of the other Medad. And the Spirit rested upon them. Now they were among those listed, but who had not gone out to the tabernacle; yet they prophesied in the camp.
27 And a young man ran and told Moses, and said, "Eldad and Medad are prophesying in the camp."
28 So Joshua the son of Nun, Moses' assistant, one of his choice men, answered and said, "Moses my lord, forbid them!"
29 Then Moses said to him, "Are you zealous for my sake? Oh, that all the LORD's people were prophets and that the LORD would put His Spirit upon them!"

Now in Numbers 11: 26-29 something interesting happens! Two men who were not of the seventy Elders by the name of Eldad and Medad received of the spirit as well and prophesied!

This is really interesting because a young man ran and told Moses that they were prophesying in the camp. Joshua who was the minister of Moses complained to Moses and said, "Eldad and Medad are prophesying in the camp, my LORD forbid them!" (verse 28)

What is interesting is that Moses answered Joshua in a profound way by saying:
"Then Moses said to him, "Are you zealous for my sake? Oh, that all the LORD's people were prophets and that the LORD would put His Spirit upon them!" Numbers 11:29 NKJV

Don't miss this important statement by Moses! It is powerful! Moses did not rebuke them or dismiss them; instead he said something that is powerful!

Moses was saying, Joshua don't be mad or envy them! Don't you think that God desires to put his spirit on everyone! It's amazing to me that there are people in the body of Christ like that young man and Joshua, who get mad because God is pouring out his spirit, and people are manifesting spiritual gifts and prophesying!

Don't get mad! Get filled with the Holy Spirit so you can manifest the gifts of the spirit as well! Moses was basically saying that there is no reason to get mad at them, because it is God's desire to fill all his people with his spirit!

There is more revelation in Numbers 11 as it relates to Moses, the 70 seventy elders, Eldad, Medad, the young man and Joshua.

Moses represents the intercessor, the prayer warrior, and prophet who stands before God and is always praying. He is also representative of the leader who cries out to the Lord for help and God sends help!

The 70 Elders represent those in ministry who have the heart of the leader and the spirit of the leader as it relates to the work of the ministry!

Eldad and Medad represent those that have the potential to lead and do the work of the ministry. Because they love the Lord, and have pure and willing hearts they are able to catch the spirit of the leadership and prophesy as well.

The young man and Joshua are representative of those that don't understand what God is doing, and always have reason to complain.

Now as it relates to Eldad and Medad, why did they catch the spirit? Here is some Biblical revelation in the Hebrew.

Eldad's name in the Hebrew means "God has loved." Medad's name in the Hebrew means "loving and affectionate." You know what the prophetic significance is? The Bible says that the spiritual gifts work through love in 1 Corinthians 13!

"And though I have the gift of prophecy, and understand all mysteries, and all knowledge; and though I have all faith, so that I could remove mountains, and have not charity (love), I am nothing." 1 Corinthians 13:2 KJV

One thing that we must understand is that spiritual gifts work through love. If you say you love God and don't love people, how can the gifts of God be manifested? There are over 300 verses of scripture in the bible that speak about love! For the sake of brevity I cannot list them all here, but here are some scriptures on the importance of walking in love:

"Hatred stirs up strife: but love covers all sins." Proverbs 10:12 KJV

"A new commandment I give unto you, that ye love one another; as I have loved you, that ye also love one another. By this shall all men know that ye are my disciples, if ye have loved one to another." John 13:34-35 KJV

"If someone says, "I love God," and hates his brother, he is a liar; for he who does not love his brother whom he has seen, how can he love God whom he has not seen? And this commandment we have from Him: that he who loves God must love his brother also." 1 John 4:20-21 NKJV

"By this we know that we love the children of God, when we love God and keep His commandments." 1 John 5:2 NKJV

Now we do know that every person that prophesies is not a prophet, nor do they have the gift of prophesy! As a matter of fact Jesus said there would be false prophets in the last days!

"And many false prophets shall rise, and shall deceive many."
Matthew 24:11 KJV

"For there shall arise false Christs, and false prophets, and shall show great signs and wonders; insomuch that, if it were possible, they shall deceive the very elect."
Matthew 24:24 KJV

Regardless of false prophets, God is raising up true prophets of God who have the spirit of Isaiah, Ezekiel, Jeremiah, Daniel, Samuel and Elijah who will speak what thus says the LORD in spirit and in truth!

The truth of the matter is that the LORD desires that all his people would be filled with the spirit and hear from heaven. Joel even confirms it in Joel 2: 28-29.

"And it shall come to pass afterward, that I will pour out my spirit upon all flesh; and your sons and your daughters shall prophesy, your old men shall dream dreams, your young men shall see visions: And also upon the servants and upon the handmaids in those days will I pour out my spirit."
Joel 2:28-29 KJV

We also need to understand that God did not intend to limit prophecy to a certain group of people. Although there are certain people that have been anointed to the office of the prophet or given the gift of prophecy. As a matter of fact, the Apostle Paul said that we should pursue spiritual gifts especially that we prophesy. Let's read!

1 Corinthians 14:1-5 NKJV
1 Pursue love, and desire spiritual gifts, but especially that you may prophesy.
2 For he who speaks in a tongue does not speak to men but to God, for no one understands him; however, in the spirit he speaks mysteries.
3 But he who prophesies speaks edification and exhortation and comfort to men.
4 He who speaks in a tongue edifies himself, but he who prophesies edifies the church.
5 I wish you all spoke with tongues, but even more that you prophesied; for he who prophesies is greater than he who speaks with tongues, unless indeed he interprets, that the church may receive edification.

Isn't this is an amazing scripture. The Apostle Paul mentions two of the spiritual gifts which are a point of contention in many denominations of the Body of Christ. Yet, Paul appears to be validating them both, especially the gift of prophecy. Although the Apostle Paul mentions it in scripture, there are still those in the body of Christ that don't receive the prophetic gift.

Prophecy is a gift that edifies, exhorts and comforts the body of Christ! God has given us this gift to bring revelation to the body, and to speak prophetically into the lives of Gods people which will not only build them up, but will comfort them and warn them.
Just as prayer is needed in these last days, we need the power of prophecy in this season like never

before. Moses is a great example of a leader who prayed with power and God used him mightily as a prophet of God.

"But since then there has not arisen in Israel a prophet like Moses, whom the LORD knew face to face."
Deuteronomy 34:10 NKJV

The Bible is full of Prophecy

All throughout the Bible we find the LORD speaking to his people through his prophets. There are many people today who don't believe that God is still speaking by his spirit to prophets.

Yes it is true that we have a more sure word of prophecy as spoken through Jesus Christ. But all throughout the Bible we find the LORD speaking prophetically to his people concerning things to come. Not only that, but he raised up men and women of God to speak and to decree his prophetic Word.

From Genesis to Revelation we find God speaking prophetically to his people starting with Adam and Eve, who disobeyed the commandment of God, and ate the forbidden fruit. After this happened, God spoke and gave them a prophetic word. (Gen 3: 14-19) When Cain killed righteous Abel, God gave him a prophetic word. (Gen 4: 10-15)

When God called Noah and brought judgement on the earth with the rain for 40 days and 40 nights. God makes a covenant with Noah and gave him a prophecy. (Gen 9: 8-17)

When God called Abraham out of his country and away from his kin folk, he gave him a prophetic word and a promise. (Gen 12: 1-4)

Even in the book of Deuteronomy, the LORD speaks prophetically through Moses and tells the people that he will raise up, and send them prophets who will speak in his name. This is how you will know if they are a true prophet sent from God.

Deuteronomy 18:18-22 NKJV
18 I will raise up for them a Prophet like you from among their brethren, and will put My words in His mouth, and He shall speak to them all that I command Him.
19 And it shall be that whoever will not hear My words, which He speaks in My name, I will require it of him.
20 But the prophet who presumes to speak a word in My name, which I have not commanded him to speak, or who speaks in the name of other gods, that prophet shall die.'
21 And if you say in your heart, 'How shall we know the word which the LORD has not spoken?'—
22 when a prophet speaks in the name of the LORD, if the thing does not happen or come to pass, that is the thing which the LORD has not spoken; the prophet has spoken it presumptuously; you shall not be afraid of him.

This is a powerful scripture that gives us a clue as to how we are to distinguish between authentic and false prophets. God gave this prophesy to Moses because the LORD was going to send many prophets to the people of God over the years, and this is how they would know the true prophets of God.

Elijah the Prophet

When we speak of the true prophets of God, It would be robbery for me to not mention one of the most bold prophets in the Bible; Elijah the Prophet. Elijah's name means "My God is Yahweh." Elijah was raised up in a time when the people were worshipping false idols and idolatry was prevalent throughout the land.

It was a time when Ahab the King of Israel and his wife Jezebel, a false prophetess were ruling in Israel. Listen to what the Bible has to say about them.

1 Kings 16:30-33 NKJV
30 Now Ahab the son of Omri did evil in the sight of the LORD, more than all who were before him.
31 And it came to pass, as though it had been a trivial thing for him to walk in the sins of Jeroboam the son of Nebat, that he took as wife Jezebel the daughter of Ethbaal, king of the Sidonians; and he went and served Baal and worshiped him.
32 Then he set up an altar for Baal in the temple of Baal, which he had built in Samaria.
33 And Ahab made a wooden image. Ahab did more to provoke the LORD God of Israel to anger than all the kings of Israel who were before him.
Yahweh raised up Elijah to prophesy against Ahab Jezebel, idolatry and false worship. The LORD clearly stated in the commandments that there should be no other gods before him!

"You shall have no other gods before me."
Exodus 20:3 NKJV

Now we see why the LORD raised up Elijah. There was so much idolatry and false worship in the land that God was going to judge it! So Elijah prophesied the Word of the LORD concerning the rain. God said because of the sin of the people lead by King Ahab and his false prophetess wife Jezebel; he was going to stop the rain. Rain was a symbol of prosperity and God's blessing. Without the rain; crops, fruits, vegetables, livestock and the people would be affected.

"And Elijah the Tishbite, of the inhabitants of Gilead, said to Ahab, "As the LORD God of Israel lives, before whom I stand, there shall not be dew or rain these years, except at my word."
1 Kings 17:1 NKJV

Elijah prayed and prophesied the Word of the LORD and stopped the rain! The Bible says that it lasted three and half years and there was a severe famine! The Apostle James in the New Testament even confirmed it.

"Elijah was a man with a nature like ours, and he prayed earnestly that it would not rain; and it did not rain on the land for three years and six months. And he prayed again, and the heaven gave rain, and the earth produced its fruit."
James 5:17-18 NKJV

To make matters worse, Obadiah, who was Ahab's servant reported to Elijah that Jezebel killed many of the LORD's prophets!

"Was it not reported to my lord what I did when Jezebel killed the prophets of the LORD, how I hid one hundred men of the LORD's prophets, fifty to a cave, and fed them with bread and water?"
1 Kings 18:13 NKJV

As a result Elijah confronted Ahab and a prophetic showdown with Jezebel's false prophets ensued. The battle took place at Mount Caramel where Elijah told Ahab to gather his false prophets, and they would see whose god was the one true God.

1 Kings 18:20-24 NKJV
20 So Ahab sent for all the children of Israel, and gathered the prophets together on Mount Carmel.
21 And Elijah came to all the people, and said, "How long will you falter between two opinions? If the LORD is God, follow Him; but if Baal, follow him." But the people answered him not a word.
22 Then Elijah said to the people, "I alone am left a prophet of the LORD; but Baal's prophets are four hundred and fifty men.
23 Therefore let them give us two bulls; and let them choose one bull for themselves, cut it in pieces, and lay it on the wood, but put no fire under it; and I will prepare the other bull, and lay it on the wood, but put no fire under it.
24 Then you call on the name of your gods, and I will call on the name of the LORD; and the God who answers by fire, He is God." So all the people answered and said, "It is well spoken."

To make a long story short, the false prophets danced, cut themselves, shouted, prophesied and nothing happened! (1 Kings 18:26-29)

Elijah then stepped up to the plate. He repaired the altar that was destroyed by the false prophets. He took twelve stones according to the twelve tribes, prepared the wood, a bull for the sacrifice, and built an altar in the name of the LORD. He then poured lots of water all over the altar. (1 Kings 18:31-35)

Elijah then called on the name of the LORD, fire fell from heaven, consumed the sacrifice, and the people of God fell on their faces, and cried out, "The LORD is God, the LORD is God! Elijah then killed all the false prophets with the sword! Let's read!

1 Kings 18:36-40 NKJV
36 And it came to pass, at the time of the offering of the evening sacrifice, that Elijah the prophet came near and said, "LORD God of Abraham, Isaac, and Israel, let it be known this day that You are God in Israel and I am Your servant, and that I have done all these things at Your word.
37 hear me, O LORD, hear me, that this people may know that you are the LORD God, and that you have turned their hearts back to you again."
38 Then the fire of the LORD fell and consumed the burnt sacrifice, and the wood and the stones and the dust, and it licked up the water that was in the trench.
39 Now when all the people saw it, they fell on their faces; and they said, "The LORD, He is God! The LORD, He is God!"
40 And Elijah said to them, "Seize the prophets of Baal! Do not let one of them escape!" So they seized them; and Elijah brought them down to the Brook Kishon and executed them there.

As a result of the miracle working power of God, Elijah turned the people's heart back to the LORD! Today's prophets will flow in the spirit of Elijah, binding and rebuking false prophets, idols, and anything that would attempt to exalt itself above the knowledge of the one true God! This is the spirit of Elijah the Prophet!

Jehoshaphat, Ahab and the False Prophets

When discussing authentic and false prophets there is a story in 1 Kings 22 that is profound. When the Kingdom was split with Israel in the North and Judah in the South, the King of Israel who was Ahab wanted to go against Syria. So he aligned himself with King Jehoshaphat who was the King of Judah. I want you to read the account here which is interesting.

1 Kings 22:1-4 NKJV
1 Now three years passed without war between Syria and Israel.
2 Then it came to pass, in the third year, that Jehoshaphat the king of Judah went down to visit the king of Israel.
3 And the king of Israel said to his servants, "Do you know that Ramoth in Gilead is ours, but we hesitate to take it out of the hand of the king of Syria?"
4 So he said to Jehoshaphat, "Will you go with me to fight at Ramoth Gilead?" Jehoshaphat said to the king of Israel, "I am as you are my people as your people, my horses as your horses."

These are interesting passages of scripture. For history sake, we all know that Ahab was a King that displeased the LORD, and Jehoshaphat was a King that pleased the LORD. They came together as allies to fight against Syria and Jehoshaphat said, before we go, let's inquire of the LORD!

1 Kings 22:5-8 NKJV
5 Also Jehoshaphat said to the king of Israel, "Please inquire for the word of the LORD today."
6 Then the king of Israel gathered the prophets together, about four hundred men, and said to them, "Shall I go against Ramoth Gilead to fight, or shall I refrain?" So they said, "Go up, for the Lord will deliver it into the hand of the king."
7 And Jehoshaphat said, "Is there not still a prophet of the LORD here, that we may inquire of Him?"
8 So the king of Israel said to Jehoshaphat, "There is still one man, Micaiah the son of Imlah, by whom we may inquire of the LORD; but I hate him, because he does not prophesy good concerning me, but evil." And Jehoshaphat said, "Let not the king say such things!"

How many of us know that this is very wise? Before we do anything in the name of the LORD we should always seek the LORD to get divine direction. Ahab was ready to go to war, but Jehoshaphat wanted to get a Word from the LORD before going to battle.

Ahab then gathered 400 false prophets and received false prophecies which were not from the LORD. Jehoshaphat discerned this and said, "Is there not a prophet of the LORD here, which we may inquire of?" This is powerful! The man of God recognized that false prophets were giving false divinations and would surely lead them to death! So he asked for a true authentic prophet of the LORD!

This blesses my heart immensely! Because in these last days there are a lot of false prophets prophesying false utterances that are not of the LORD! We need the true authentic prophets of the LORD to give us divine direction from the LORD in these last days!

What is even more interesting is that Ahab said, "Yes we have another prophet, but I hate him, because he never speaks anything good concerning me." Did you hear what he just said?

"So the king of Israel said to Jehoshaphat, "There is still one man, Micaiah the son of Imlah, by whom we may inquire of the LORD; but I hate him, because he does not prophesy good concerning me, but evil." And Jehoshaphat said, "Let not the king say such things!"
1 Kings 22:8 NKJV

When you read the remaining passages of scripture from 1 Kings 22: 13-28, the Prophet Micaiah does not agree with the 400 false prophets of Ahab and prophesies that if they go to war they will be succeed!

"Therefore look! The LORD has put a lying spirit in the mouth of all these prophets of yours, and the LORD has declared disaster against you."
1 Kings 22:23 NKJV

True Prophets of God will not align themselves with evil. They will say exactly what the LORD says! We must never align ourselves with anyone who goes against the Word of God. We must stand firm on the commandments of God no matter what people say or think!

Anybody can say the LORD said this or that, but we need to hear from the true prophets of God who have the heart of God, the spirit of God and who desire to do the will of God!

There are four Major Prophets in the Bible that I want to briefly discuss. Their prophecies were very important not only for the Old Testament Saints, but for the New Testament as well! The prophets I am referring to are Isaiah, Jeremiah, Ezekiel and Daniel.

Isaiah the Prophet

Isaiah is recognized as one of the greatest prophets of the Bible. He was called to prophesy to the nations of Israel, Judah and the surrounding nations. He was also called to prophesy concerning the coming of the Messiah Jesus Christ! Many of us have read about Isaiah and his prophecies. One of the most familiar prophecies is in Isaiah 9.

Isaiah 9:6-7 NKJV
6 For unto us a Child is born, unto us a Son is given; and the government will be upon His shoulder. And His name will be called Wonderful, Counselor, Mighty God, Everlasting Father, Prince of Peace.
7 Of the increase of His government and peace there will be no end, upon the throne of David and over His kingdom, to order it and establish it with judgment and justice from that time forward, even forever. The zeal of the Lord of hosts will perform this.

Jesus even quoted Isaiah in the New Testament during his earthly ministry.

Matthew 15:7-9 MKJV
7 Hypocrites! Well did Isaiah prophesy of you, saying,
8 This people draw near to me with their mouth, and honor me with their lips, but their heart is far from me.
9 But in vain they worship me, teaching for doctrines the commandments of men."

As a matter of fact when Jesus launched into his ministry after overcoming the devils temptations in the desert, he went into the temple, and read from the book of Isaiah about his own ministry and life.

Luke 4:14-21 NKJV
14 Then Jesus returned in the power of the Spirit to Galilee, and news of Him went out through all the surrounding region.
15 And He taught in their synagogues, being glorified by all.
16 So He came to Nazareth, where He had been brought up. And as His custom was, He went into the synagogue on the Sabbath day, and stood up to read.
17 And He was handed the book of the prophet Isaiah. And when He had opened the book, He found the place where it was written:
18 The spirit of the LORD is upon me, because he has anointed me to preach the Gospel to the poor. He has sent me to heal the brokenhearted, and to proclaim liberty to the captives and recovery of sight to the blind. To set at liberty those who are oppressed;
19 To proclaim the acceptable year of the LORD.
20 Then He closed the book, and gave it back to the attendant and sat down. And the eyes of all who were in the synagogue were fixed on Him.

21 And He began to say to them, "Today this Scripture is fulfilled in your hearing."

Isaiah was truly an anointed Prophet whose words are powerful and encourage us today!

Jeremiah the Weeping Prophet

Jeremiah the Prophet was raised up by the LORD to prophesy to Judah concerning their destruction by Nebuchadnezzar and their seventy years of captivity. Jeremiah was called the weeping prophet because his message was constantly rejected by the people.

It saddened his heart that they did not receive God's Word. He also wrote the book of Lamentations which is a collection of poetic laments for the destruction of Jerusalem, and the despair of the people of Judah for the loss of their land, city and temple.

Jeremiah 25:1-11 NKJV
1 The word that came to Jeremiah concerning all the people of Judah, in the fourth year of Jehoiakim the son of Josiah, king of Judah (which was the first year of Nebuchadnezzar king of Babylon),
2 which Jeremiah the prophet spoke to all the people of Judah and to all the inhabitants of Jerusalem, saying:
3 "From the thirteenth year of Josiah the son of Amon, king of Judah, even to this day, this is the twenty-third year in which the word of the LORD has come to me; and I have spoken to you, rising early and speaking, but you have not listened.
4 And the LORD has sent to you all His servants the prophets, rising early and sending them, but you have not listened nor inclined your ear to hear.

5 They said, 'Repent now every one of his evil way and his evil doings, and dwell in the land that the LORD has given to you and your fathers forever and ever.

6 do not go after other gods to serve them and worship them, and do not provoke me to anger with the works of your hands; and I will not harm you.'

7 Yet you have not listened to me," says the LORD, "that you might provoke me to anger with the works of your hands to your own hurt.

8 Therefore thus says the LORD of hosts: 'Because you have not heard my words,

9 behold, I will send and take all the families of the north,' says the LORD, 'and Nebuchadnezzar the king of Babylon, My servant, and will bring them against this land, against its inhabitants, and against these nations all around, and will utterly destroy them, and make them an astonishment, a hissing, and perpetual desolations.

10 Moreover I will take from them the voice of mirth and the voice of gladness, the voice of the bridegroom and the voice of the bride, the sound of the millstones and the light of the lamp.

11 And this whole land shall be desolation and astonishment, and these nations shall serve the king of Babylon seventy years.

What is amazing is that when Jerusalem and Judah were taken into captivity, the LORD did not allow them to take Jeremiah the Prophet!

Jeremiah 40:2-4 NKJV

2 And the captain of the guard took Jeremiah and said to him: "The LORD your God has pronounced this doom on this place.

3 Now the LORD has brought it, and has done just as

He said. Because you people have sinned against the LORD, and not obeyed His voice, therefore this thing has come upon you.

4 And now look, I free you this day from the chains that were on your hand. If it seems good to you to come with me to Babylon, come, and I will look after you. But if it seems wrong for you to come with me to Babylon, remain here. See, all the land is before you; wherever it seems good and convenient for you to go, go there."

Ezekiel Prophesies to the Dry Bones

There is a powerful story in the Bible about the prophet Ezekiel who is told by the LORD to prophesy to a valley of dry bones to bring them to life. Ezekiel obeys the LORD and prophesies to the dry bones! After dry bones come together, he is told to prophesy again to the wind to bring breath life to the dry bones! This is a powerful story concerning the nation of Israel! Let's read!

Ezekiel 37:1-14 NKJV
1 The hand of the LORD came upon me and brought me out in the Spirit of the LORD, and set me down in the midst of the valley; and it was full of bones.
2 Then He caused me to pass by them all around, and behold, there were very many in the open valley; and indeed they were very dry.
3 And He said to me, "Son of man, can these bones live?" So I answered, "O Lord GOD, You know."
4 Again He said to me, "Prophesy to these bones, and say to them, 'O dry bones, hear the word of the LORD!
5 Thus says the Lord GOD to these bones: "Surely I will cause breath to enter into you, and you shall live.

6 I will put sinews on you and bring flesh upon you, cover you with skin and put breath in you; and you shall live. Then you shall know that I am the LORD."
7 So I prophesied as I was commanded; and as I prophesied, there was a noise, and suddenly a rattling; and the bones came together, bone to bone.
8 Indeed, as I looked, the sinews and the flesh came upon them, and the skin covered them over; but there was no breath in them.
9 Also He said to me, "Prophesy to the breath, prophesy, son of man, and say to the breath, 'Thus says the Lord GOD: "Come from the four winds, O breath, and breathe on these slain, that they may live."
10 So I prophesied as He commanded me, and breath came into them, and they lived, and stood upon their feet, an exceedingly great army.
11 Then He said to me, "Son of man, these bones are the whole house of Israel. They indeed say, 'Our bones are dry, our hope is lost, and we ourselves are cut off!'
12 Therefore prophesy and say to them, 'Thus says the Lord GOD: "Behold, O My people, I will open your graves and cause you to come up from your graves, and bring you into the land of Israel.

As we can see God used his prophets time and time again to prophesy concerning the Nation of Israel and Judah. This is a powerful story of how God uses prophets to decree and declare his Word to resurrect, bring life and restoration to his people!

Daniel, Beloved in the sight of the LORD

What more could be say about Daniel the Prophet who was taken captive by Babylon as a young Hebrew slave during the destruction of the temple at Jerusalem. Daniel was faithful all his days to the LORD. The Bible says that Daniel was beloved in the sight of the LORD.

"At the beginning of your prayers the commandment came out, and I have come to explain. **For you are greatly beloved;** therefore understand the matter, and attend to the vision."
Daniel 9:23 NKJV

"And he said to me, O Daniel, **a man greatly beloved**, understand the words that I speak to you, and stand upright. For to you I am now sent. And when he had spoken this word to me, I stood trembling."
Daniel 10:11 NKJV

"And said, **O man greatly beloved**, do not fear. Peace to you; be strong; yes, be strong. And when he had spoken to me, I was made stronger, and I said, speak my lord, for you have made me stronger."
Daniel 10:19 NKJV

Daniel was the last of the four Major Prophets, but his prophetic ministry was powerful. Many believers, who are familiar with end time prophecy, know that some of Daniels prophecies confirm what is written in the book of Revelation.

Daniel was not only a prophet but he was a prayer warrior and intercessor as well. When they tried to set a trap for Daniel to not pray according to the law of the Medes and Persians. Daniel prayed to the God of Abraham, Isaac and Jacob as he always did!

Daniel 6:10-11 NKJV
10 Now when Daniel knew that the writing was signed, he went home. And in his upper room, with his windows open toward Jerusalem, he knelt down on his knees three times that day, and prayed and gave thanks before his God, as was his custom since early days.
11 Then these men assembled and found Daniel praying and making supplication before his God.

Daniel 9:2-5 NKJV
2 in the first year of his reign I, Daniel, understood by the books the number of the years specified by the word of the LORD through Jeremiah the prophet, that He would accomplish seventy years in the desolations of Jerusalem.
3 Then I set my face toward the Lord God to make request by prayer and supplications, with fasting, sackcloth, and ashes.
4 And I prayed to the LORD my God, and made confession, and said, "O Lord, great and awesome God, who keeps His covenant and mercy with those who love Him, and with those who keep His commandments,
5 we have sinned and committed iniquity, we have done wickedly and rebelled, even by departing from your precepts and your judgments.

Daniel was truly a beloved prophet of the LORD We can learn a lot from Daniel in ministry today. Daniel did not compromise. He was faithful, he had an excellent spirit, and no error or fault was found in him. In other words, Daniel was a righteous servant and man of God.

"So the governors and satraps sought to find some charge against Daniel concerning the kingdom; but they could find no charge or fault, because he was faithful; nor was there any error or fault found in him."
Daniel 6:4 NKJV

Daniel was so beloved in the sight of the LORD that the LORD spoke to Ezekiel who prophesied about Noah, Daniel and Job as righteous men! This is truly awesome!

Ezekiel 14:12-14 NKJV
12 The word of the LORD came again to me, saying:
13 "Son of man, when a land sins against Me by persistent unfaithfulness, I will stretch out My hand against it; I will cut off its supply of bread, send famine on it, and cut off man and beast from it.
14 Even if these three men, Noah, Daniel, and Job, were in it, they would deliver only themselves by their righteousness," says the Lord GOD.

This is truly a powerful scripture. God used Noah, Daniel and Job as examples of righteousness!

Samuel, Deborah, Huldah and Joel

There are other prophets who spoke powerfully and prophetically in the name of the LORD as well. Samuel was one of the first Old Testament prophets. He anointed the first King of Israel, Saul. He also anointed the greatest King of Israel, King David, who was a man after God's heart. Samuel was so anointed that none of his prophecies fell to the ground. What he prophesied came to pass!

"So Samuel grew, and the LORD was with him and let none of his words fall to the ground."
1 Samuel 3:19 NKJV

Deborah was a Prophetess who was also a judge. Deborah is an interesting individual because she is the only female prophet who was also a judge in the Old Testament. She was so anointed that when it was time for war, the men would not go without her!

Judges 4:4-8 NKJV
4 Now Deborah, a prophetess, the wife of Lapidoth, was judging Israel at that time.
5 And she would sit under the palm tree of Deborah between Ramah and Bethel in the mountains of Ephraim. And the children of Israel came up to her for judgment.
6 Then she sent and called for Barak the son of Abinoam from Kedesh in Naphtali, and said to him, "Has not the LORD God of Israel commanded, 'Go and deploy troops at Mount Tabor; take with you ten thousand men of the sons of Naphtali and of the sons of Zebulun;
7 and against you I will deploy Sisera, the commander of Jabin's army, with his chariots and his multitude at the River Kishon; and I will deliver him into your hand'?"
8 And Barak said to her, "If you will go with me, then I will go; but if you will not go with me, I will not go!"

There was another female Prophet in the Bible as well. Her name is Huldah. Many people are not familiar with her. She prophesied to King Josiah concerning the destruction that would come to Judah because of their idolatry.

She said that his life would be spared because of his tender heart toward the LORD!

2 Kings 22:14-19 NKJV
14 So Hellish the priest, Ahikam, Achbor, Shaphan, and Asaiah went to Huldah the prophetess, the wife of Shallum the son of Tikvah, the son of Harhas, keeper of the wardrobe. (She dwelt in Jerusalem in the Second Quarter.) And they spoke with her.
15 Then she said to them, "Thus says the LORD God of Israel, 'Tell the man who sent you to me,
16 Thus says the LORD: 'Behold, I will bring calamity on this place and on its inhabitants—all the words of the book which the king of Judah has read—
17 because they have forsaken me and burned incense to other gods, that they might provoke me to anger with all the works of their hands. Therefore my wrath shall be aroused against this place and shall not be quenched.
18 But as for the king of Judah, who sent you to inquire of the LORD, in this manner you shall speak to him, 'Thus says the LORD God of Israel: "Concerning the words which you have heard—
19 because your heart was tender, and you humbled yourself before the LORD when you heard what I spoke against this place and against its inhabitants, that they would become a desolation and a curse, and you tore your clothes and wept before Me, I also have heard you," says the LORD.

Josiah was a righteous King who followed in the footsteps of David. Because of his righteous ways, God prophesied that he would not see judgment!

Joel prophesied concerning the judging of nations, the day of the LORD, and that the LORD would pour out his spirit in the last days.

"And it shall come to pass afterward That I will pour out My Spirit on all flesh; Your sons and your daughters shall prophesy, Your old men shall dream dreams, Your young men shall see visions. And also on my menservants and on my maidservants I will pour out My Spirit in those days."
Joel 2:28-29 NKJV

On the day of Pentecost, when the Holy Spirit came with power, the Apostle Peter confirmed it in the book of Acts 2: 16-18

Acts 2:16-18 NKJV
16 But this is that which was spoken by the prophet Joel:
17 And it shall be in the last days, says God, I will pour out of My Spirit upon all flesh. And your sons and your daughters shall prophesy, and your young men shall see visions, and your old men shall dream dreams.
18 And in those days I will pour out My Spirit upon menservants and woman servants, and they shall prophesy.

We could go on and on discussing the prophets of God, but it would take pages to discuss them all. We have listed only a handful of the Prophets of the Bible in this book, but you can read about many of the Minor Prophets in the Bible as well, such as Amos, Jonah, Haggai, Malachi and many more. They all spoke powerful prophecies in the name of the LORD.

We also cannot fail to mention the Gospels in which Jesus prophesied about the end times, and the book of Revelation which conveys a blessing upon all those read, hear, and keep the things which are written in it.

"Blessed is he that reads, and they that hear the words of this prophecy, and keep those things which are written therein, for the time is at hand."
Revelation 1:3 KJV

God throughout history has spoken his Word to his people by his prophets. Even in the last days the Father has spoken by his Son, the greatest prophet of all; Jesus Christ.

Jesus the Greatest Prophet

All throughout scripture there is no greater prophet that has arisen than the LORD Jesus Christ. All throughout the Gospels we find Jesus speaking prophetically to the people of that day. He also prophesied concerning the destruction of the temple.

Matthew 24:1-2 NKJV
1 Then Jesus went out and departed from the temple, and His disciples came up to show Him the buildings of the temple.
2 And Jesus said to them, "Do you not see all these things? Assuredly, I say to you, not one stone shall be left here upon another, that shall not be thrown down."

Jesus also prophesied about the end times before his return.

Matthew 24:3-8 NKJV
3 Now as He sat on the Mount of Olives, the disciples came to Him privately, saying, "Tell us, when will these things be? And what will be the sign of Your coming, and of the end of the age?"
4 And Jesus answered and said to them: "Take heed that no one deceives you.
5 For many will come in My name, saying, 'I am the Christ,' and will deceive many.
6 And you will hear of wars and rumors of wars. See that you are not troubled; for all these things must come to pass, but the end is not yet.
7 For nation will rise against nation, and kingdom against kingdom. And there will be famines, pestilences, and earthquakes in various places.
8 All these are the beginning of sorrows.

One of the most profound prophetic stories in the Gospels is in the book of John chapter 4. Jesus and the disciples are traveling to Galilee and passing through Samaria. Jesus is tired and wearied from his journey, and takes a break at a water well while the disciples go into town to buy food.

John 4:5-8 NKJV
5 So He came to a city of Samaria which is called Sychar, near the plot of ground that Jacob gave to his son Joseph.
6 Now Jacob's well was there. Jesus therefore, being wearied from His journey, sat thus by the well. It was about the sixth hour.
7 A woman of Samaria came to draw water. Jesus said to her, "Give Me a drink."
8 For His disciples had gone away into the city to buy food.

It is at this well in Samaria where Jesus meets a woman. As they converse, Jesus prophesies about her life which amazes the woman. Her response is profound!

John 4:9-14 NKJV
9 Then the woman of Samaria said to Him, "How is it that you, being a Jew, ask a drink from me, a Samaritan woman?" For Jews have no dealings with Samaritans.
10 Jesus answered and said to her, "If you knew the gift of God, and who it is who says to you, 'Give Me a drink,' you would have asked Him, and He would have given you living water."
11 The woman said to Him, "Sir, You have nothing to draw with, and the well is deep. Where then do You get that living water?
12 Are You greater than our father Jacob, who gave us the well, and drank from it himself, as well as his sons and his livestock?"
13 Jesus answered and said to her, "Whoever drinks of this water will thirst again,
14 but whoever drinks of the water that I shall give him will never thirst. But the water that I shall give him will become in him a fountain of water springing up into everlasting life."

As the woman attempts to school Jesus about the well in which they are drawing the water. Jesus tells her something profound about living water.

"Jesus answered and said to her, "Whoever drinks of this water will thirst again, but whoever drinks of the water that I shall give him will never thirst. But the water that I shall give him will become in him a fountain of water springing up into everlasting life."

John 4:13-14 NKJV

The woman responds by saying:
"Sir, give me this water that I may not thirst, nor come here to draw." John 4:15 NKJV

Jesus then prophesies about her past and current life and her response in verse 19 is profound:

John 4:16-19 NKJV
16 Jesus said to her, "Go, call your husband, and come here."
17 The woman answered and said, "I have no husband." Jesus said to her, "You have well said, 'I have no husband,'
18 for you have had five husbands, and the one whom you now have is not your husband; in that you spoke truly."
19 The woman said to Him, "Sir, I perceive that You are a prophet.

They continue to converse as Jesus gives her a powerful prophetic word about true worship. This is a Word that each and every believer should receive and understand!

John 4:23-24 NKJV
23 But the hour is coming, and now is, when the true worshipers will worship the Father in spirit and truth; for the Father is seeking such to worship Him.
24 God is Spirit, and those who worship Him must worship in spirit and truth."

The end of the conversation deals with prophecies concerning the coming of the Messiah in which the woman was aware of. Jesus last words to her are very prophetic as he tells her that all the prophecies spoken are all about me!

John 4:25-26 NKJV
25 The woman said to Him, "I know that Messiah is coming" (who is called Christ). "When He comes, He will tell us all things."
26 Jesus said to her, "I who speak to you am He."

As a result of this prophetic encounter, this woman's life was changed and she evangelized her whole city and told them about Jesus the Messiah! (John 4: 28-30)

There is so much more that we could say about Jesus Christ, the Son of God who was the greatest prophet that ever walked this earth. Everything he did was prophetic and miraculous. There is truly no one like him that ever walked this earth. The prophetic words spoken by Moses are ever so true.

"The LORD your God will raise up for you a Prophet like me from your midst, from your brethren. Him you shall hear."
Deuteronomy 18:15 NKJV

Out of all the prophets that were raised up from the nation of Israel, Jesus Christ, the Son of the living God fulfilled all the prophecies spoken by the prophets of old. He was truly the one prophet that each and every one of us should have an ear to hear in these last days. (Rev 3: 6)

The Apostle Paul and Prophecy

The Apostle Paul had a lot to say about prophecy as

well. Many believers love prayer and praise, but for some reason they don't like to talk much about prophecy. To deny prophecy in scripture would be to deny the Bible because the majority of the Bible is full of prophets, prophecy and prophetic events.

What I like about the Apostle Paul is that he was truly a spiritual man who had the heart of Christ. Paul understood spiritual and heavenly things so he was fully qualified to talk about prophecy and its importance. Some of the most profound scriptures in the Bible concern spiritual gifts. Everyone in the Body of Christ should know about the spiritual gifts of 1 Corinthians chapter 12. Paul gives an amazing discourse on spiritual gifts and prophecy as it relates to the New Testament church. Let's read!

1 Corinthians 12:3-11 KJV
3 Wherefore I give you to understand, that no man speaking by the Spirit of God calls Jesus accursed: and that no man can say that Jesus is the Lord, but by the Holy Ghost.
4 Now there are diversities of gifts, but the same Spirit.
5 And there are differences of administrations, but the same Lord.
6 And there are diversities of operations, but it is the same God which works all in all.
7 But the manifestation of the Spirit is given to every man to profit withal.
8 For to one is given by the Spirit the word of wisdom; to another the word of knowledge by the same Spirit;
9 To another faith by the same Spirit; to another the gifts of healing by the same Spirit;
10 To another the working of miracles; to another

prophecy; to another discerning of spirits; to other different kinds of tongues; to another the interpretation of tongues:
11 But all these work that one and the selfsame Spirit, dividing to every man severally as he will.

Paul in his discourse concerning spiritual gifts says that in the Body of Christ each person has been given a spiritual gift. Just as God gives us natural gifts when we were born, he gives us spiritual gifts when we are born again of his spirit. There are nine spiritual gifts and they are:

1. The word of wisdom
2. The word of knowledge
3. Faith
4. Gifts of healing
5. Working of miracles
6. Prophecy
7. Discerning of Spirits
8. Different kinds of tongues
9. Interpretation of tongues

Each and every believer in Christ has been given a spiritual gift or gifts. It is not my intention to explain or go into a discourse on the spiritual gifts, but notice that prophecy is listed as a spiritual gift. What is amazing to me is that there are people in the Body of Christ that do not accept some of these gifts. Paul's teaching is balanced, profound and gives us wisdom concerning these God given spiritual gifts.

1 Corinthians 12:27-31 KJV
27 Now ye are the body of Christ, and members in particular.
28 And God hath set some in the church, first

apostles, secondarily prophets, thirdly teachers, after that miracles, then gifts of healings, helps, governments, diversities of tongues.

29 Are all apostles? are all prophets? are all teachers? are all workers of miracles?

30 Have all the gifts of healing? do all speak with tongues? do all interpret?

31 But covet earnestly the best gifts: and yet shew I unto you a more excellent way.

Did you read what Paul said? We are the Body of Christ and members! He goes on to add that God has set some in the church, first apostles, second prophets, third; teachers, miracles, gifts of healing, helps, governments, and different kinds of tongues.

Now the wisdom in this passage of scripture is that Paul asks the question? Are all apostles, prophets, teachers, and he asks the same question of other gifts as well. Paul is saying that although God has blessed us with spiritual gifts, not everyone has these particular gifts, but it is alright to desire these gifts!

This is the balance and wisdom that I want to bring from scripture. Not everyone is an Apostle, not everyone is a Prophet, and everyone does not have all of the gifts. Notice the language that Paul uses in verse 28, "And God has set some in the church!" Some is defined as; an unspecified amount or number of, or a considerable amount or number of.

My purpose here is not to debate the spiritual gifts or who has them, but to show you that the Apostle Paul who wrote the majority of the New Testament books by the spirit of God in Jesus name recognized the spiritual gifts, especially prophecy!

Paul doesn't stop there. He brings balance to the gifts by saying:

1 Corinthians 13:1-2 KJV
1 Though I speak with the tongues of men and of angels, and have not charity, I am become as sounding brass, or a tinkling cymbal.
2 And though I have the gift of prophecy, and understand all mysteries, and all knowledge; and though I have all faith, so that I could remove mountains, and have not charity, I am nothing.

Sometimes we elevate the spiritual gifts to a higher degree than we should. Don't get me wrong. Spiritual gifts are very important for the church and Body of Christ, but the most important thing to have is love!

Paul goes even deeper concerning two of the most controversial gifts in the church; tongues and prophecy! What I love about God is that his Words are spirit and they are life. He will give us the truth and clarity that we need to be balanced.   In 1 Corinthians 14, Paul goes even deeper and gives us great wisdom.

1 Corinthians 14:1-4 KJV
1 Follow after charity (love), and desire spiritual gifts, but rather that ye may prophesy.
2 For he that speaks in an unknown tongue speaks not unto men, but unto God: for no man understands him; howbeit in the spirit he speaks mysteries.
3 But he that prophesies speaks unto men to edification, and exhortation, and comfort.
4 He that speaks in an unknown tongue edifies himself; but he that prophesies edifies the church.

Did you hear that? Follow after love and desire spiritual gifts, but I would rather that you prophesy! For he that speaks in an unknown tongue speaks not unto men but to God. But he that prophesies speaks unto men, edification, exhortation and comfort! Not only that, but he that speaks in tongues edifies himself, but prophesies edifies the church!

Wow! This is powerful teaching from the Apostle Paul. If the church would follow scripture and what has been written to us from one of the greatest servants of the LORD, we would have less confusion and more power in our churches among the believers in Christ! As you can see, prophesy is very important to us, not only in the Old Testament, but the New Testament as well.

Saints, we should never minimize spiritual gifts, especially the gift of prophecy that has been given to us by the LORD.

CHAPTER 4

THE POWER OF PRAISE IN SCRIPTURE

Psalms 150:1-6 NKJV
1 Praise the LORD! Praise God in His sanctuary;
Praise Him in His mighty firmament!
2 Praise Him for His mighty acts; Praise Him
according to His excellent greatness!
3 Praise Him with the sound of the trumpet; Praise
Him with the lute and harp!
4 Praise Him with the timbrel and dance; Praise Him
with stringed instruments and flutes!
5 Praise Him with loud cymbals; Praise Him with
clashing cymbals!
6 Let everything that has breath praise the LORD.
Praise the LORD!

One of the things that we see all throughout
scripture is praise. I don't believe there is a book in
the Bible where we don't read about someone giving
God praise! This is an area in our relationship with
the LORD that is not optional. Why? Because the
Bible continuously exhorts us to praise the LORD!

As a matter of fact Jesus told the religious leaders of
that day that if the people didn't praise him, the rocks
would cry out! Let's read!

Luke 19:37-40 KJV
37 And when he was come nigh, even now at the
descent of the mount of Olives, the whole multitude
of the disciples began to rejoice and praise God with
a loud voice for all the mighty works that they had
seen;

38 Saying Blessed be the King that cometh in the name of the Lord: peace in heaven, and glory in the highest.

39 And some of the Pharisees from among the multitude said unto him, Master, rebuke thy disciples.

40 And he answered and said unto them, I tell you that, if these should hold their peace, the stones would immediately cry out.

In Luke chapter 19, the Pharisees wanted Jesus to rebuke the disciples because they were praising and magnifying the LORD! But Jesus response is profound, because he said, "If they hold their peace, the stones would cry out!"

I don't know about you, but I don't want rocks crying out on my behalf! Why? Because God is great and greatly to be praised, and he has been good to each and every one of us! When we think about it, there is something that each and every one of us can give God glory and praise for!

We must understand that God's presence and power is manifested when we are all on one accord as it relates to powerful praise and worship! In Psalm 150 verse 6, we find the Psalmist exclaiming the power of praise and the last verse is powerful: "Let everything that has breath praise the LORD!"

Psalms 150:1-6 NKJV
1 Praise the LORD! Praise God in His sanctuary; Praise Him in His mighty firmament!
2 Praise Him for His mighty acts; Praise Him according to His excellent greatness!
3 Praise Him with the sound of the trumpet; Praise

Him with the lute and harp!
4 Praise Him with the timbrel and dance; Praise Him with stringed instruments and flutes!
5 Praise Him with loud cymbals; Praise Him with clashing cymbals!
6 Let everything that has breath praise the LORD. Praise the LORD!

Many of us have been in churches where we get a praise break and there is shouting, leaping, jumping, singing and the power of Holy Spirit is present, but what would you do if there was no musician present?

Listen to what Hebrews 13:15 says:
"Therefore by Him let us continually offer the sacrifice of praise to God, that is, the fruit of our lips, giving thanks to His name."
Hebrews 13:15 NKJV

Did you get that last line of Hebrews 13: 15? Let us offer the sacrifice of praise to God continually, that is, the fruit of our lips giving thanks to his name.

How many of us know that offering God starts with a sacrifice. A sacrifice is giving something up that belongs to you. A sacrifice is something that you give, even when you don't have it to give. Sometimes we don't feel like praising, but God deserves the praise! As a matter of fact, can you give God praise when the money is funny! Can you give God praise when you have family situations or a job situation going on? Maybe this is why David could say in Psalm 34:1:

"I will bless the LORD at all times; His praise shall continually be in my mouth."
Psalms 34:1 NKJV

Regardless of what we go through in life, God deserves the praise, because he is able to make all grace abound toward us!

In Psalm 8: 1-2, King David is exclaiming the excellence of God and says something so profound in verse 2.

"Out of the mouth of babes and nursing infants You have ordained strength, because of Your enemies, that You may silence the enemy and the avenger." Psalms 8:2 NKJV

There are many commentaries concerning this scripture, but the revelation of it is that David is magnifying the LORD and uses this occasion to say; even the babes and nursing infants understand the power and strength of opening their mouths to loudly exclaim that which they need from their parents! In the Hebrew, the word "Strength" "is oze" which means praise, force, security, majesty, boldness, loud, might, and strong.

So in actuality when we open our mouth and begin to praise the LORD, force, majesty, might and strength is released. This is the power of our praise! Because the Bible says when praise, strength, majesty and might are released, we will silence the avenger.

Think about this for a moment. When you are going through, the natural response is to be discouraged, disappointed, or dismayed. But the supernatural response is praise and to rejoice, which stills or stops the avenger who is the enemy or adversary! The way that we get the victory in every area of our life is through our praise!

Praise is good for us because it allows us the opportunity to thank the LORD, and to bless his name for who he is, and what he has done for us through his blood at the cross of Calvary. It also gives us the opportunity to show how much we love him and appreciate him.

Let me ask you a question? When something awesome happens in your life what is your response? When you get a promotion on your job what is your response? When God opens the windows of heaven and pours you out a blessing, what is your response? If someone were to put $1000.00 in your hand right now, what would be your response? The answer to these questions is to give God praise!

Even if something significant does not happen in your life, God still deserves the praise, and has already blessed us with all spiritual blessings in heavenly places according to his Word.

"Blessed be the God and Father of our Lord Jesus Christ, who has blessed us with every spiritual blessing in the heavenly places in Christ."
Ephesians 1:3 NKJV

Sometimes we wait for the blessing or breakthrough to manifest before we praise God, but we must always praise and thank him by faith! The Bible says that God has already blessed us with every spiritual blessing in heavenly places!

So truth be told, God has already done it, and if he doesn't do another thing, we are already blessed high and above measure! So I encourage you to have the spirit of David and say by faith:

"I will bless the LORD at all times: his praise shall continually be in my mouth. My soul shall make her boast in the LORD: the humble shall hear thereof, and be glad. O magnify the LORD with me, and let us exalt his name together."
Psalms 34:1-3 KJV

Paul and Silas Praying and Praising

There is a very interesting story as it relates to prayer, prophecy and praise in the book of Acts. The Apostle Paul and his traveling companion Silas were led by the spirit to go to Macedonia. The Bible says that as they were going to pray, they met a slave girl who was possessed with a spirit of divination, who brought her masters profit by fortune telling. Let's read!

Acts 16:16-24 NKJV
16 Now it happened, as we went to prayer, that a certain slave girl possessed with a spirit of divination met us, who brought her masters much profit by fortune-telling.
17 This girl followed Paul and us, and cried out, saying, "These men are the servants of the Most High God, who proclaim to us the way of salvation."
18 And this she did for many days. But Paul, greatly annoyed, turned and said to the spirit, "I command you in the name of Jesus Christ to come out of her." And he came out that very hour.

As Paul and Silas were going to a place of prayer, they came upon a woman who was possessed by a spirit of divination that prophesied through her. Now understand that the enemy will also use false prophetic utterances as well.

Someone once asked me, "What is the difference between a prophet and a psychic?" The response was; a prophet tells you what is on God's mind. A psychic tells you what is on your mind. The difference is the spirit from where the utterance or word proceeds from. God uses prophets, and the devil uses psychics."

So this girl began to follow Paul and Silas and recognized the spirit of God that was upon them. She began to follow them and began to mock them by crying out (verse 17) "These men are the servants of the Most High God, who proclaim to us the way of salvation."

The Bible says that she did this for many days and it irritated Paul because he knew that it was not a genuine spirit. It was a mocking spirit from hell that was sent to distract them. The Bible says that Paul then cast the spirit out of her!

"And this she did for many days. But Paul, greatly annoyed, turned and said to the spirit, "I command you in the name of Jesus Christ to come out of her." And he came out that very hour."
Acts 16:18 NKJV

After Paul cast out the spirit, the masters of the slave girl were upset and had Paul and Silas thrown into prison, where they were beaten with rods, and locked up with chains.

Acts 16:19-24 NKJV
19 But when her masters saw that their hope of profit was gone, they seized Paul and Silas and dragged them into the marketplace to the authorities.
20 And they brought them to the magistrates, and said, "These men, being Jews, exceedingly trouble our city;
21 and they teach customs which are not lawful for us, being Romans, to receive or observe."
22 Then the multitude rose up together against them; and the magistrates tore off their clothes and commanded them to be beaten with rods.

23 And when they had laid many stripes on them, they threw them into prison, commanding the jailer to keep them securely.
24 Having received such a charge, he put them into the inner prison and fastened their feet in the stocks.

Now understand that Paul and Silas were only trying to get to a place of prayer and the enemy came against them. Isn't it amazing that whenever you are ready to pray, you get sleepy, the phone rings, or someone texts you! These are distractions!

As a result, they were falsely accused of causing trouble, and teaching customs not lawful, and thrown into prison and locked up. While Paul and Silas were in prison after being falsely accused, this didn't stop them from praising God.

Acts 16:25-31 NKJV
25 But at midnight Paul and Silas were praying and singing hymns to God, and the prisoners were listening to them.
26 Suddenly there was a great earthquake, so that the foundations of the prison were shaken; and immediately all the doors were opened and everyone's chains were loosed.
27 And the keeper of the prison, awaking from sleep and seeing the prison doors open, supposing the prisoners had fled, drew his sword and was about to kill himself.
28 But Paul called with a loud voice, saying, "Do yourself no harm, for we are all here."
29 Then he called for a light, ran in, and fell down trembling before Paul and Silas.
30 And he brought them out and said, "Sirs, what must I do to be saved?"

31 So they said, "Believe on the Lord Jesus Christ, and you will be saved, you and your household."

The Bible says at midnight, after being beaten and locked up, that Paul and Silas began praying and singing hymns to God. In other words they were praying and praising God! Not only that, but the prisoners were listening to them.

The Bible says that all of a sudden, there was an earthquake and the foundations of the prison were shaken and the doors and chains of all the prisons were loosed! Let's read Acts 16 verse 26!

26 Suddenly there was a great earthquake, so that the foundations of the prison were shaken, and immediately all the doors were opened, and everyone's chains were loosed.

The Bible says as a result of this miracle, the jailer was saved and came to know Jesus Christ as LORD!

"And he brought them out and said, "Sirs, what must I do to be saved?" So they said, "Believe on the Lord Jesus Christ, and you will be saved, you and your household."
Acts 16:30-31 NKJV

This is an amazing story and guess what, it all started with prayer and praise! I want you to know that despite what you go through in life, prayer and praise makes the difference! Remember that the power of prayer and praise will loose your chains, change your situation and bring you victory in Jesus name!

Jesus and the Tribe of Judah

As we discuss the power of praise, we cannot overlook the significance of the tribe of Judah. Jesus descended from the tribe of Judah, and Judah in the Hebrew means "Praise." In the Bible, Jesus is also called the Lion of the Tribe of Judah.

"But one of the elders said to me, "Do not weep. Behold, **the Lion of the tribe of Judah**, the Root of David, has prevailed to open the scroll and to loose its seven seals."
Revelation 5:5 NKJV

Many of the victorious Kings that we read about in scripture were also from the Tribe of Judah. We find that some of the Kings from the Tribe of Judah were also Kings that did what was right in the sight of the LORD. They were; Asa, Jehoshaphat, Uzziah, Hezekiah, and Josiah and last but definitely not least David, the sweet Psalmist of Israel who was a man after God's heart. (2 Sam 23: 1)

King David himself was a Psalmist and loved music. He wrote many of the Psalms that we read in scripture today. Many of the Psalms were about the greatness and excellence of God, praise, worship, victory over enemies, humility, deliverance, cries and prayers for help, thanking God for his love, kindness, and compassion. David even prayed and praised God for Israel and Jerusalem.

Psalms 122:1-9 NKJV
1 A Song of Ascents of David. I was glad when they said to me, "Let us go into the house of the LORD."
2 Our feet have been standing Within your gates, O

Jerusalem!

3 Jerusalem is built As a city that is compact together,

4 Where the tribes go up, The tribes of the LORD, To the Testimony of Israel, To give thanks to the name of the LORD.

5 For thrones are set there for judgment, The thrones of the house of David.

6 Pray for the peace of Jerusalem: "May they prosper who loves you.

7 Peace be within your walls, Prosperity within your palaces."

8 For the sake of my brethren and companions, I will now say, "Peace is within you."

9 Because of the house of the LORD our God I will seek your good.

Remember we said that praise is important for us because it gives us the opportunity to magnify and thank God for who he is, and what he has done at the cross on our behalf. It also gives us the opportunity to show how much we love him and appreciate him.

Praise also allows us the opportunity to exalt, magnify, thank, and lift up the name of Jesus! This can be through music, the lifting of hands, and from the fruit of our lips with love and heartfelt praise.

In order for us to get a greater understanding of praise, there are four Hebrew words for praise that I want to share. Due to the large number of scriptures in the Bible, we will only list a few examples here.

1. Halal - is a primary Hebrew root word for praise. Our word "hallelujah" comes from this base word.

It means to be clear, to shine, to boast, show, to rave, celebrate, and to be clamorously foolish."

Psalm 69:30 "I will praise (halal) the name of God with a song, and will magnify him with thanksgiving."

Psalm 69:34 "Let the heaven and earth praise (halal) him, the seas, and everything that moves therein."

2. Yadah - is a verb with a root meaning; the extended hand, to throw out the hand, to hold out the hands, and also to worship with extended hand.

2Ch 20:21 "And when he had consulted with the people, he appointed singers unto the LORD, and that should praise the beauty of holiness, as they went out before the army, and to say, Praise (yadah) the LORD; for his mercy endures forever."

Ps 107:15 "Oh that men would praise (yadah) the Lord for his goodness, and for his wonderful works to the children of men."

3. Towdah - comes from the same principle root word as yadah, but is used more specifically. Towdah literally means an extension of the hand in adoration, avowal, or acceptance.

Ps 50:14 "Offer unto God praise (Towdah) and pay thy vows unto the Most High."

Ps 50:23 "Whoso offers praise (Towdah) glorifies me, and to him that orders his conversation aright will I shew the salvation of God."

4. Shabach – means to shout, or address in a loud tone, to command, and to triumph.

Ps 47:1 "O clap your hands, all peoples; shout (Shabach) to God with the voice of joy (or triumph)."

Ps 145:4 "One generation shall praise (Shabach) thy works to another and declare thy mighty acts."

Isa 12:6 "Cry aloud and shout (Shabach) for joy, O inhabitant of Zion, for great in your midst is the Holy One of Israel."

What we must understand is that praise is supernatural. In these last days, the power of prayer, prophecy and praise will be the vehicle that will SHIFT the body of Christ to new levels of God's glory, power, presence and provision! These three powerful spiritual weapons will stifle the enemy and give us great victory in Jesus Name!

In order for us to manifest the power of prayer, prophecy and praise, we must open our mouths and lift up our voices like a trumpet. There is a profound scripture in the Psalms that confirms this.

Psalms 81:10-13 KJV
10 I am the LORD thy God, which brought thee out of the land of Egypt: open thy mouth wide, and I will fill it.
11 But my people would not hearken to my voice; and Israel would none of me.
12 So I gave them up unto their own hearts' lust: and they walked in their own counsels.
13 Oh that my people had hearkened unto me, and Israel had walked in my ways!

The Psalmist says in Psalm 81 that when the LORD bought the children of Israel out of Egypt, he told them to open their mouths wide and he would fill it.

God was looking for them to open their mouth to pray and praise his Most High Name because of the great things he had done! Yet the scripture says that they would not hearken to his voice. Instead of using their mouths to pray and praise God, they walked in their own counsels, and used their mouths to murmur and complain!

This is why you must open your mouth and keep praising God despite everything you go through! Stop looking at your bank account and start praying, stop looking at your current situation and start prophesying, stop looking at your circumstances and start praising, because your breakthrough is in your praise, your blessing is in your praise, your healing is in your praise, and your financial breakthrough is in your praise! Open your mouth wide says the LORD and I will fill it!

What we are believing and trusting God will only manifest when we open our mouths by faith in the name of Jesus! When we open our mouths to pray, prophesy and praise, we are coming into agreement with what the LORD has already predestined, purposed, promised and prophesied according to the scripture. Isaiah confirms this by prophesying the words of Jesus Christ:

Isaiah 61:1-3 KJV
1 The Spirit of the Lord GOD is upon me; because the LORD hath anointed me to preach good tidings unto the meek; he hath sent me to bind up the

brokenhearted, to proclaim liberty to the captives, and the opening of the prison to them that are bound;
2 To proclaim the acceptable year of the LORD, and the day of vengeance of our God; to comfort all that mourn;
3 To appoint unto them that mourn in Zion, to give unto them beauty for ashes, the oil of joy for mourning, the garment of praise for the spirit of heaviness; that they might be called trees of righteousness, the planting of the LORD, that he might be glorified.

Did you hear that? Jesus is able to bring freedom, deliver, heal the broken hearted, set the captives free, release the prisoners, comfort those that mourn, give beauty for ashes, the oil of gladness for mourning, and above all, the garment of praise for the spirit of heaviness!

Jesus said the Spirit of the LORD is upon me and I am anointed to bring deliverance and salvation to all those that need it. I will bring salvation, deliverance, health and wholeness to all who will receive it, and break the spirit of heaviness, replacing it with the spirit of praise! Praise God!

Hallelujah to the name of Jesus! Let's take a moment and give God a hallelujah praise! Hallelujah in the Hebrew means "Praise the LORD!" It is also the highest praise one can render to the LORD! Open your mouth and shout hallelujah, and give God the highest praise that is due his Most High name!

CHAPTER 5

A THREEFOLD CORD FOR VICTORY: PRAYER, PROPHECY AND PRAISE

Ecclesiastes 4:9-12 NKJV

9 Two are better than one, Because they have a good reward for their labor.

10 For if they fall, one will lift up his companion. But woe to him who is alone when he falls, for he has no one to help him up.

11 Again, if two lie down together, they will keep warm; But how can one be warm alone?

12 Though one may be overpowered by another, two can withstand him. And a threefold cord is not quickly broken.

In the book of Ecclesiastes, Solomon the wise man exclaims the wisdom and power of unity. He states that two are better than one, and that a threefold cord is not easily broken. What does this mean?

Solomon is giving us the wisdom of strength and unity in numbers. In verse 9, he says that two are better than one! We know this to be true, because if you had to lift something heavy, and it was too much for you. You would call someone to assist you to get it moved!

He further adds that if one be overpowered, two can

withstand it, and a threefold cord, or the power of three is not easily broken! We all know that prayer is powerful alone, but when prophecy is added there is much more power. Yet, when prayer, prophecy and praise are utilized together, it is not easily broken. It is a powerful threefold cord for victory in Jesus Name. In other words victory is sure!

I mentioned earlier that the Bible is full of prayer, prophecy and praise. Whenever we see these powerful principles used in scripture victory was certain! Every time we read about prayer, prophecy and praise in scripture, God always gave his people victory! These biblical principles are powerful and give us supernatural power in the midst of a spiritual battle!

One of the most profound examples of prayer, prophecy and praise can be found in the Old Testament, in the book of 2 Chronicles chapter 20, verses 1-30. It is the story of Jehoshaphat, one of the righteous Kings who descended from the Tribe of Judah. In this story we see the power of prayer, prophecy and praise which gave them absolute victory over the enemy. Let's read!

Jehoshaphat's Victory

One of the most powerful stories in scripture that give us great examples of prayer, prophecy and praise as a threefold cord for victory can be found in 2 Chronicles chapter 20. This is a powerful story that many of us can relate too. Many of us can attest and agree that sometimes life just happens. We can be living our life free from worry, sickness and pain and then all of a sudden, something out of the ordinary happens. It could be a financial situation, a family situation, or even a sickness or marriage situation. Regardless of what it is, life sometimes happens and it will come in the form of trials, tribulations, troubles and tragedies.

This is exact what happened to King Jehoshaphat, but God him victory through prayer, prophecy and praise! As I share this story, commentary will be provided so that we get the full revelation of the story.

The Exposition of 2 Chronicles 20: 1: 30

2 Chron 20:1 It happened after this that the people of Moab with the people of Ammon, and others with them besides the Ammonites, came to battle against Jehoshaphat.

During the reign of Jehoshaphat, King of Judah, there arose a situation beyond the Kings control. Three enemies of Israel came together to battle against them. We all know that battles can come in the form of trials, tribulations, troubles, and attacks from the devil, and no one is exempt from them. Many times we have to deal with one enemy, but as we see, sometimes multiple enemies will

band together to come against us, and their only desire is to defeat and destroy us!

2 Chron 20:2 Then some came and told Jehoshaphat, saying, "A great multitude is coming against you from beyond the sea, from Syria; and they are in Hazazon Tamar" (which is En Gedi).

One of the things I thank God for is people who are watchmen. They watch the back of the leadership! There were some people who came and told the King that three enemies were about to attack and they were on the move against Jehoshaphat! Even in our lives, sometimes we get negative reports and bad news from a doctor, a friend, family member, a bill, or even a phone call.

2 Chron 20:3 And Jehoshaphat feared, and set himself to seek the LORD, and proclaimed a fast throughout all Judah.

The Bible says that Jehoshaphat heard the news and feared. Although God has not given us the spirit of fear, there are times when we receive news or a report that just startles us. Anybody ever been there?

That's why we must watch what we hear, because negative reports can cause us to fear at times. Even when you are going through a situation, fear or worry can grip you and overtake you. Although the King feared, he began to pray and seek the LORD, and proclaimed a fast throughout all of Judah! This is profound, because although we may fear, we turn our face toward heaven to seek the LORD!

Remember Jesus said in Matthew 17:20-21, there are some mountains that can be moved with your faith, and some mountains, situations, circumstances or demonic activity that can only be removed by prayer and fasting!

Matthew 17:20-21 NKJV
20 So Jesus said to them, "Because of your unbelief; for assuredly, I say to you, if you have faith as a mustard seed, you will say to this mountain, 'Move from here to there,' and it will move; and nothing will be impossible for you.
21 However, this kind does not go out except by prayer and fasting."

The Bible says that Jehoshaphat set himself to seek the LORD, and proclaimed a fast throughout Judah. In other words, it wasn't just him and his family. It was the whole Kingdom of Judah. How many of us know there are personal fasts, and there are corporate fasts, in which we need everyone to be on one accord. Why? Because there is strength in unity and numbers!

2 Chron 20:4 So Judah gathered together to ask help from the LORD; and from all the cities of Judah they came to seek the LORD.

The people unified and gathered together to ask help from the Lord and they all came together in unity. This is very important. Remember what David said in Psalm 133:1: "Behold, how good and how pleasant it is For brethren to dwell together in unity!" Psalms 133:1 NKJV

We must always remember that when we unify we are stronger! No man or woman is an island!

2 Chron 20:5 Then Jehoshaphat stood in the assembly of Judah and Jerusalem, in the house of the LORD, before the new court,
2 Chron 20:6 and said: "O LORD God of our fathers, are You not God in heaven, and do You not rule over all the kingdoms of the nations, and in Your hand is there not power and might, so that no one is able to withstand You?

The King went to the house of God, the Temple, and stood before the LORD in prayer. As he began to pray, he acknowledged the LORD as the God of our fathers, and great God in heaven who rules over all kingdoms of the nations.

He reminded God that he is awesome and great with all power in his hand and that no one can withstand or defeat him. He did this in the form of questions? "Lord is it not true that you have all power and might in your hands, so that no one can withstand you?"

The Bible says in Heb 4:16, "Let us therefore come boldly to the throne of grace, that we may obtain mercy and find grace to help in time of need." You can sense the boldness that is with Jehoshaphat. As he went into the House of God, in the presence of God, he went humbly but boldly as if he were presenting his case before the Righteous Judge of heaven and earth!

We must always remember that God has given us the ability to come boldly into his presence, because he is truly a righteous judge who will render and give us justice against our adversary!

Jesus told the story of a woman in Luke 18 who had a complaint against her adversary and she went boldly to the judge and got what she wanted from the LORD!

Luke 18:7 "And shall God not avenge His own elect who cry out day and night to Him, though He bears long with them?"

In other words the LORD was saying if an unjust judge will render justice and give you what you desire, how much more will God do who is a Righteous Judge!

2 Chron 20:7 Are You not our God, who drove out the inhabitants of this land before your people Israel, and gave it to the descendants of Abraham Your friend forever?

The King is glorying God and reminding him of his covenant promises to the children of Israel, who are the descendants of Abraham, to whom the Promised Land was given. He even name dropped Abraham! Why did he do that? Because God made a covenant promise with Abraham, and Jehoshaphat knew that God keeps and honors his Word!
As a matter of fact, we need to remember those covenant promises belong to us as well. Listen to the Apostle Paul:

Gal 3:29 And if you are Christ's, then you are Abraham's seed, and heirs according to the promise.

What were those promises made to Abraham and his seed? Well, let's read Gen 22: 16-18. Jehoshaphat is literally reminding God of all he said to Father Abraham!

Gen 22:16 and said: "By Myself I have sworn, says the LORD, because you have done this thing, and have not withheld your son, your only son—
Gen 22:17 blessing I will bless you, and multiplying I will multiply your descendants as the stars of the heaven and as the sand which is on the seashore; and your descendants shall possess the gate of their enemies.
Gen 22:18 In your seed all the nations of the earth shall be blessed, because you have obeyed My voice."

Jehoshaphat knew the word and he reminded the LORD of the covenant promises made. This is important for us to remember. Because Jesus Christ is the same yesterday, today and forevermore! We should always remind God of his promises to us in his Word, and pray his Word! Why? Because God honors his Word!

**"I will worship toward Your holy temple, And praise Your name For Your lovingkindness and Your truth; For You have magnified Your word above all Your name."
Psalms 138:2 NKJV**

**"So shall My word be that goes forth from My mouth; It shall not return to Me void, But it shall accomplish what I please, And it shall prosper in the thing for which I sent it."
Isaiah 55:11 NKJV**

2Ch 20:8 and they dwell in it, and have built you a sanctuary in it for your name, saying,

2Ch 20:9 'If disaster comes upon us—sword, judgment, pestilence, or famine—we will stand before this temple and in Your presence (for Your name is in this temple), and cry out to You in our affliction, and You will hear and save.'

He then goes on to say that we have built you a wonderful sanctuary and you have given us a promise, but the enemy desires to destroy us! LORD you said in your Word, if we stand in this temple and sanctuary in your presence and cry out, you will hear from heaven and save us. LORD you said that you would protect us from sword, judgement, pestilence and famine. So LORD, we cry out to you in our affliction to hear from heaven to save us!

2 Chron 20:10 And now, here are the people of Ammon, Moab, and Mount Seir, whom You would not let Israel invade when they came out of the land of Egypt, but they turned from them and did not destroy them.

He calls the enemy by name; Ammon, Moab and Mount Seir. How many or us know that you have to know who your enemy is and call that strong man spirit by name as you wage warfare!

As a matter of fact, what are the enemies that

are coming to defeat you? Discouragement, despair, division, dissension, discord, doubt, or depression? We must know who our enemy is, and in order to defeat them we must destroy every demon and devil that comes against us in Jesus name!

2 Chron 20:11 here they are, rewarding us by coming to throw us out of Your possession which You have given us to inherit.

He also says that the LORD showed them mercy many years ago, but here they are now coming against us. I want to say this is the importance of spiritual warfare and deliverance! Anytime we wage warfare in the spirit, we want to rebuke, bind, cast out and destroy every demon and devil in hell. Why? They might come back against us!

How many of us know that the enemy wants to destroy the mission, and mandate which God has given to us. The enemy wants to kill, steal and destroy purpose, dreams, and visions that the Lord has given to us. There are some things that God has purposed for us to inherit, but the enemy wants to keep us from it.

2 Chron 20:12 O our God, will you not judge them? For we have no power against this great multitude that is not coming against us; nor do we know what to do, but our eyes are upon You."

He asks the Lord to judge them because this enemy or situation is greater than what he can handle. Jesus said that the widow in Luke chapter 18 asked the judge to grant her justice against her adversary. How many of us know that the LORD will grant us our requests because he is truly a Righteous Judge!

2 Tim 4:8   refers to the Lord as the righteous Judge. Rev 19:2 says, He is true and righteous are His judgments. Rev 19:11 says, that in righteousness He judges and makes war.

The King then humbles himself and says, "Lord we don't know what to do, but our eyes are on you." This is so profound! Because the scripture tells us in Psalm 121: 1; I will lift up mine eyes unto the hills, from where comes my help. Hebrews 12:2 says, "Looking unto Jesus the author and finisher of our faith. When we don't know what to do, we must look to heaven for divine assistance!

2 Chron 20:13 Now all Judah, with their little ones, their wives, and their children, stood before the LORD.

Notice all of the people and their families stood before the Lord. The Bible says their little ones, wives and children. In other words, little Billy had to get off PlayStation and little Suzy had to put her phone down to come to prayer with the rest of the family.

What would happen if we stopped making excuses and we all got on one accord in agreement and unity and pressed our way to prayer. What would happen if churches, families, and friends got on one accord?

Jesus said in Luke 11:23, He who is not with me is against me, and he who does not gather with me scatters. There are moments in life when we must come together in complete unity and agreement to accomplish a goal.

Jesus said "Again I say to you that if two of you agree on earth concerning anything that they ask, it will be done for them by My Father in heaven. For where two or three are gathered together in My name, I am there in the midst of them."
Matthew 18:19-20 NKJV

2 Chron 20:14 Then the Spirit of the LORD came upon Jahaziel the son of Zechariah, the son of Benaiah, the son of Jeiel, the son of Mattaniah, a Levite of the sons of Asaph, in the midst of the assembly.

This is powerful! After they came together in unity, prayed and fasted, the LORD spoke through a prophet by the name of Jahaziel.

2 Chron 20:15 And he said, "Listen, all you of Judah and you inhabitants of Jerusalem, and you, King Jehoshaphat! Thus says the LORD to you: 'Do not be afraid or dismayed because of this great multitude, for the battle is not yours, but God's.

Did you hear that? After prayer came a prophecy! The LORD spoke directly to the inhabitants of Jerusalem and Judah. The prophet said, "Don't fear and don't be dismayed." Dismayed means to be discouraged or terrified because of how big, or how great the situation is. Nevertheless the LORD said, "Because the battle is not yours but God's."

The Word God in verse 15 is (Elohim) It refers to a magistrate or Supreme God, a Great God, or judge who is mighty. The LORD literally said, "I got your back and the battle is mines not yours."

2 Chron 20:16 Tomorrow go down against them. They will surely come up by the Ascent of Ziz, and you will find them at the end of the brook before the Wilderness of Jeruel.

Isn't it profound that the LORD gives them a

powerful prophetic word, and tells them exactly where the enemy is, and what they must do to engage the enemy.

2 Chron 20:17 You will not need to fight in this battle. Position yourselves, stand still and see the salvation of the LORD, who is with you, O Judah and Jerusalem!' Do not fear or be dismayed; tomorrow go out against them, for the LORD is with you."

Did you hear that? It's not our battle. You will not need to fight in this battle! Why, because God will fight for us. He is Jehovah Nissi – our banner. We must position ourselves. We must stand still; stop running to and fro, so that we can see the salvation of the LORD! The LORD said don't fear and don't be dismayed! Go out against them, for I AM with you!

The scripture says in Psalm 46:10, Be still, and know that I am God: I will be exalted among the heathen; I will be exalted in the earth.

Exo 14:14 says, "The LORD shall fight for you, and you shall hold your peace."

We do not need to fear. God has not given us the spirit of fear but of power love and a sound mind. David said, "Yea though we walk through the valley of death we shall fear no

evil."

2 Chron 20:18 And Jehoshaphat bowed his head with his face to the ground, and all Judah and the inhabitants of Jerusalem bowed before the LORD, worshiping the LORD.

After praying to the LORD, a prophecy comes forth with a word of revelation for victory. He then bows down and worships the LORD! As a result everyone bows down and begins to worship the Lord in spirit and in truth and in the beauty of his holiness! This is powerful! When the people of God saw their leader bow in worship, they began to bow down and worship as well!

2 Chron 20:19 Then the Levites of the children of the Kohathites and of the children of the Korahites stood up to praise the LORD God of Israel with voices loud and high.

Did you see what just transpired? There was prayer, prophecy and praise! After they had prayed, the LORD gave them a powerful prophetic Word, and they praised God with a loud, radical praise!

2 Chron 20:20 So they rose early in the morning and went out into the Wilderness of Tekoa; and as they went out, Jehoshaphat stood and said, "Hear me, O Judah and you inhabitants of Jerusalem: Believe in

the LORD your God and you shall be established; believe His prophets, and you shall prosper."

The King then goes before the people in boldness. Remember in verse 3 he feared. But now since he has gotten a prophetic Word from the LORD, he is standing in faith with boldness exclaiming, "Believe in the LORD your God, and you shall be established. Believe his prophets and you shall prosper!" Wow, in other words, God has spoken and we have the victory!

Jesus said in Matt 10: 41, "He who receives a prophet in the name of a prophet shall receive a prophet's reward. And he who receives a righteous man in the name of a righteous man shall receive a righteous man's reward."

Question, do you believe the word of God? Are you standing on the promises of God? Heb 4:2 says "For unto us was the gospel preached, as well as unto them: but the word preached did not profit them, not being mixed with faith in them that heard it."

People of God, whatever God has said in his word shall come to pass. The Bible says that faith comes by hearing, and hearing by the Word of God. (Rom 10: 17) Jehoshaphat prayed, a prophetic word came forth, the people received it by faith and they praised

God!

2 Chron 20:21 and when he had consulted with the people, he appointed those who should sing to the LORD, and who should praise the beauty of holiness, as they went out before the army and were saying: "Praise the LORD, For His mercy endures forever."

He then consults with the people and appointed the true praisers. Isn't that amazing? Sometimes you got to take inventory of what you have and select some true warriors, true watchmen, true intercessors, and prayer warriors you can count on who understand the power of prayer, prophecy and praise.

Isn't it profound that as they were going to the battle, they did not put their special warfare warriors on the front line. They put the praise team on the front line to lead the people to victory in the battle.

This was truly supernatural. Because any General will tell you in time of war, you don't put the Navy, Army, and Airforce band on the front line. You put your special warfare teams on the front line who are skilled and prepared for battle! Yet, the LORD, said put the radical praisers on the front line!

What is even more amazing is that the

**praisers were given instructions to go out
before the army and say, "Praise the LORD,
for His mercy endures forever!" I want you to
read this again. They were to go out to meet
the enemy and their battle cry was "Praise the
LORD, for His mercy endures forever!"**

2 Chron 20:22 Now when they began to sing and to
praise, the LORD set ambushes against the people of
Ammon, Moab, and Mount Seir, who had come
against Judah; and they were defeated.

**The scripture says as they began to sing and
praise, the enemy was defeated! Let me
repeat that! As they began to sing and praise,
the enemy was defeated! As they began to sing
and praise, the Lord caused the enemy to set
ambushes against one another and they were
defeated!**

2 Chron 20:23 for the people of Ammon and Moab
stood up against the inhabitants of Mount Seir to
utterly kill and destroy them. And when they had
made an end of the inhabitants of Seir, they helped to
destroy one another.

**So as they sang and praised, the LORD set the
enemy against himself and they began to kill
and destroy one another. This was truly
supernatural and only God could cause this to
happen.**

2 Chron 20:24 So when Judah came to a place overlooking the wilderness, they looked toward the multitude; and there were their dead bodies, fallen on the earth. No one had escaped.

When the battle was over, Judah (Praise) overlooked the wilderness and there was a multitude of dead bodies of the enemy everywhere!

People of God, this is what happens when you unify in prayer. God sends a prophetic word of knowledge to give you divine direction and when we praise, the end result is victory!

2 Chron 20:25 When Jehoshaphat and his people came to take away their spoil, they found among them an abundance of valuables on the dead bodies, and precious jewelry, which they stripped off for themselves, more than they could carry away; and they were three days gathering the spoil because there was so much.

The Bible says that when Jehoshaphat and the people came to take away the spoil, they found an abundance of valuables and precious jewelry on the dead bodies of the enemy. They stripped off the valuables from the enemy and the Bible says they were three days gathering the goods from the enemy because there was so much! Say what?

This is truly an amazing story in which we see prayer, prophecy and praise in effect as a threefold cord which gave them the victory. All of this happened as a result of unity, prayer, fasting, and seeking the LORD. As a result, God spoke through a prophet and released a divine praise strategy for victory and they were blessed high and above measure!

2 Chron 20:26 And on the fourth day they assembled in the Valley of Berachah, for there they blessed the LORD; therefore the name of that place was called The Valley of Berachah until this day.

2 Chron 20:27 Then they returned, every man of Judah and Jerusalem, with Jehoshaphat in front of them, to go back to Jerusalem with joy, for the LORD had made them rejoice over their enemies.

2 Chron 20:28 So they came to Jerusalem, with stringed instruments and harps and trumpets, to the house of the LORD.

2 Chron 20:29 And the fear of God was on all the kingdoms of those countries when they heard that the LORD had fought against the enemies of Israel.

2 Chron 20:30 Then the realm of Jehoshaphat was quiet, for his God gave him rest all around.

Verses 26 – 30 say they assembled in the valley of Berachah and rejoiced in the LORD because they got the victory. This is an interesting passage of scripture because the word Berachah in the Hebrew means "blessing." So they literally assembled in

valley of blessing and blessed the LORD!

They returned to the House of the LORD in Jerusalem and continued to praise God with instruments, and the fear of God was on all the nations when they heard the LORD gave them victory. The Bible then says that God gave them rest all around.

This is truly an amazing story of victory and it all started with prayer, prophecy and praise! This is an excellent example of what happens when we stand on the spiritual principles found in the Word of God!

We see the power of prayer, prophecy and praise gave the people victory, and guess what? Whatever spiritual battles that you may have, God will certainly give you the victory as well!

Throughout this book we have looked at the power of prayer, prophecy and praise, but we have not scratched the surface in all that the Bible has to say about each one of these biblical principles. I encourage you to go even deeper in your study concerning these powerful Biblical principles.

Word of Encouragement

In these last days, every believer must have the spirit of David which is a worshipper and warrior!

Psalm 144:1, A Psalm of David. "Blessed be the LORD

my strength, which teaches my hands to war, and my fingers to fight."
One of the things we must never forget is that there is an unseen war raging in the spirit realm. Light against darkness, good against evil, godliness against ungodliness and angels against demons!

Just because you don't see it in the natural, it is going on spiritually in the unseen realm! We know it to be so because the Apostle Paul told us in Ephesians 6:12, "For we do not wrestle against flesh and blood, but against principalities, against powers, against the rulers of the darkness of this age, against spiritual hosts of wickedness in the heavenly places."

All throughout the Bible we see Israel fighting enemies. Paul even said that we should fight the good fight of faith in 1Tim 6:12, "Fight the good fight of faith, lay hold on eternal life, to which you were also called and have confessed the good confession in the presence of many witnesses."

There are many reading this that may say, "Pastor I don't like to fight and I don't want to fight!" Well my dear brother and sister, I have to tell you that although we didn't start the fight, the enemy will bring the fight against your church, marriage, ministry, health, family, finances, and your life! The devil often picks fights with us even when we don't want a fight! Maybe that's why David said in, Psalm 144:1, A Psalm of David. "Blessed be the LORD my strength, which teaches my hands to war, and my fingers to fight."

Although the battle is already won and we have the victory in Jesus Name, we still have to walk it out in the physical realm. Although we are meek and walk in peace, we should have the mindset of David who said that the Most High God himself teaches me how to war, and my fingers to fight. God himself will give us the wisdom in this spiritual battle!

Who are we fighting? Against the wicked one, against the forces of darkness, and against anything that would exalt itself against the Word of God! We don't fight with natural weapons; we war in the spirit with prayer, prophecy and praise!

The scripture says in 2 Cor 10:3-4 "For though we walk in the flesh, we do not war after the flesh: For the weapons of our warfare are not carnal, but mighty through God to the pulling down of strong holds."

Today ask God to give you the heart of a warrior and worshipper with a powerful prayer voice to prophesy the Word of God with power, and a radical praise that will still and stop the devil in his tracks!

To conclude, I have provided multiple scriptures on prayer, prophecy and praise to encourage you in your study. Due to the extensive number of scriptures in the Bible concerning these powerful principles, I have provided a short list of these scriptures.

My prayer is that whatever you go through in life, you will always stand strong in faith through prayer, prophecy and praise to get the victory in Jesus Name! God Bless!

Scriptures on Prayer

Psalm 5:3 My voice shalt thou hear in the morning, O LORD; in the morning will I direct my prayer unto thee, and will look up.

Matt 17:21 Howbeit this kind goes not out but by prayer and fasting.

Matt 21:13 And said unto them, It is written, My house shall be called the house of prayer; but ye have made it a den of thieves.

Matt 21:22 And all things, whatsoever ye shall ask in prayer, believing, ye shall receive.

Luk 6:12 Now it came to pass in those days that He went out to the mountain to pray, and continued all night in prayer to God.

Luk 19:46 saying to them, "It is written, 'My House is a House of Prayer,' but you have made it a 'den of thieves. "

Act 6:4 But we will give ourselves continually to prayer, and to the ministry of the word.

Eph 6:18 praying always with all prayer and supplication in the Spirit, being watchful to this end, with all perseverance and supplication for all the saints.

Phil 4:6 Be careful for nothing; but in everything by prayer and supplication with thanksgiving let your requests be made known unto God.

Jam 5:15 And the prayer of faith shall save the sick, and the Lord shall raise him up; and if he have committed sins, they shall be forgiven him.

Jam 5:16 Confess your faults one to another, and pray one for another, that ye may be healed. The effectual fervent prayer of a righteous man avails much.

1 Pet 4:7 But the end of all things is at hand: be ye therefore sober, and watch unto prayer.

Scriptures on Prophecy

Rom 12:6 Having then gifts differing according to the grace that is given to us, whether prophecy; let us prophesy according to the proportion of faith.

1 Cor 12:10 to another the working of miracles; to another prophecy; to another discerning of spirits; to another divers kinds of tongues; to another the interpretation of tongues:

1 Cor 13:2 And though I have the gift of prophecy, and understand all mysteries, and all knowledge; and though I have all faith, so that I could remove mountains, and have not charity, I am nothing.

1 Tim 4:14 Neglect not the gift that is in thee, which was given thee by prophecy, with the laying on of the hands of the presbytery.

2 Pet 1:20 Knowing this first, that no prophecy of the scripture is of any private interpretation.

2 Pet 1:21 For the prophecy came not in old time by the will of man: but holy men of God spoke as they were moved by the Holy Ghost.

Rev 1:3 Blessed is he that reads and they that hear the words of this prophecy, and keep those things which are written therein: for the time is at hand.

Rev 19:10 And I fell at his feet to worship him. And he said unto me, See thou do it not: I am thy fellowservant, and of thy brethren that have the testimony of Jesus: worship God: for the testimony of Jesus is the spirit of prophecy.

Rev 22:7 Behold, I come quickly: blessed is he that keeps the sayings of the prophecy of this book.

Rev 2:10 And he said unto me, Seal not the sayings of the prophecy of this book: for the time is at hand.

Rev 22:18 For I testify unto every man that hears the words of the prophecy of this book, If any man shall add unto these things, God shall add unto him the plagues that are written in this book:

Rev 22:19 And if any man shall take away from the words of the book of this prophecy, God shall take away his part out of the book of life, and out of the holy city, and from the things which are written in this book.

Scriptures on Praise

Psalm 9:2 I will be glad and rejoice in thee. I will sing praise to thy name, O thou most High.

Psalm 28:7 The LORD is my strength and my shield; my heart trusted in him, and I am helped: therefore my heart greatly rejoices; and with my song will I praise him.

Psalm 34:1 I will bless the LORD at all times; His praise shall continually be in my mouth.

Psalm 56:4 In God I will praise his word, in God I have put my trust; I will not fear what flesh can do unto me.

Psalm 56:10 In God will I praise his word: in the LORD will I praise his word.

Psalm 66:2 Sing forth the honor of his name: make his praise glorious.
Psalm 67:3 Let the people praise thee, O God; let all the people praise thee.

Psalm 98:4 Make a joyful noise unto the LORD, all the earth: make a loud noise, and rejoice, and sing praise.

Psalm 100:1 A Psalm of praise. Make a joyful noise unto the LORD, all ye lands.

Psalm 100:4 Enter into his gates with thanksgiving, and into his courts with praise: be thankful unto him, and bless his name.

Psalm 107:8 Oh that men would praise the LORD for his goodness, and for his wonderful works to the children of men!

Psalm 149:1 Praise ye the LORD. Sing unto the LORD a new song, and his praise in the congregation of saints.

Psalm 150:1 Praise ye the LORD. Praise God in his sanctuary: praise him in the firmament of his power.

Psalm 150:2 Praise him for his mighty acts: praise him according to his excellent greatness.

Psalm 150:6 Let everything that hath breath praise the LORD. Praise you the LORD.

Jer 17:14 Heal me, O LORD, and I shall be healed; save me, and I shall be saved: for thou art my praise.

Matt 21:16 And said unto him, Have you heard what these say? And Jesus said unto them, Yea; have ye never read, Out of the mouth of babes and nursing infants thou hast perfected praise?

Heb 13:15 By him therefore let us offer the sacrifice of praise to God continually, that is, the fruit of our lips giving thanks to his name.

Rev 19:5 Then a voice came from the throne, saying, "Praise our God, all you His servants and those who fear Him, both small and great!"

Here is how you can receive Jesus Christ as Lord and Savior:

1. Admit your need (I am a sinner).
2. Be willing to turn from your sins (Repent of your sins).
3. Pray and believe in your heart and confess with your mouth that Jesus Christ is Lord. (Believe and receive Jesus Christ as Lord and Savior)
4. Be baptized in the Name of Jesus for the remission of your sins and you shall receive the gift of the Holy Spirit. (Be filled with the Holy Spirit)

How to Pray:

Heavenly Father, I come to you in the Name of Jesus. I confess and repent of my sins. I believe in my heart and confess with my mouth that Jesus is Lord. I believe that you died on the cross for my sins. You were buried and resurrected on the third day. Come into my heart and life. Fill me with your precious Holy Spirit. Today I believe, trust and follow Jesus Christ as my Lord and Savior. In Jesus Name! Amen.

This is just the beginning of a wonderful new life in Jesus Christ. To deepen this relationship you should:

Read your Bible every day to know Christ better. Communicate and talk to God in prayer every day. Tell others about Christ. Worship, fellowship, and serve with other born again Spirit filled Christians in a church where Christ, and the true Gospel is preached. As Christ's representative in the world, demonstrate your new life by your love and concern for others. The Bible says, "Let your light so shine, that others may see your good works and glorify your Father in heaven. Matt 5: 16.

About the Author

Pastor Jamal E. Quinn is the Senior Pastor of Firm Foundation Christian Fellowship in Riverview, FL. He is a native of Louisville, Kentucky and a U.S. Navy veteran of 21 years.

He accepted the call into the ministry and was licensed as a Minister of the Gospel of Jesus Christ in 1999. In May 2002 - 2003, while serving in the military he was ordered to the Middle East with Special Operations Command Central Forward on a one-year assignment in Doha, Qatar. It was at this time while serving in the desert, that the Lord called him to preach the Gospel and minister the Word of God in True Righteousness, Holiness, Deliverance and Truth.

In June 2003, he was assigned to Naval Air Station Jacksonville, Florida on another assignment. During this time he committed himself to a thorough and diligent study of the Holy Bible. In September of 2005, he retired after serving 21 years in the U.S. Navy.

In Oct 2005, he returned home to Riverview, Florida where the Lord led him to start a community Bible study by faith. Preaching and teaching the Gospel in his neighborhood to anyone that had an ear to hear. In Oct 2007, after faithfully conducting a Bible study group in his home, the Lord called Pastor Jamal and Prophetess Sheryl Quinn to plant Firm

Foundation Christian Fellowship in the community of Riverview.

Pastor Quinn is a visionary, shepherd, and watchman who preaches the Gospel of the Kingdom with passion, power and truth. Pastor Quinn's passion is teaching, exhorting and encouraging the Body of Christ to fulfill their God ordained destiny, and to live their lives as examples in Jesus Christ.

He received his Associate of Science Degree at Excelsior College, Albany, New York, and obtained his Bachelor of Arts in Pastoral Ministry from South Florida Bible College and Theological Seminary in Deerfield Beach, FL.

Pastor Quinn has been married to Co-Pastor and 1st Lady Sheryl Quinn, his high school sweetheart for 34 years. For additional information on Pastor Quinn or other books, visit https://jamalquinn.com/
For additional information on Firm Foundation Christian Fellowship, visit https://www.firmfoundationcf.org

www.ingramcontent.com/pod-product-compliance
Lightning Source LLC
Chambersburg PA
CBHW071552040426
42452CB00008B/1147